Information
Nation

Information Nation

Seven Keys to Information Management Compliance

Second Edition

Randolph A. Kahn
Barclay T. Blair

WILEY

Wiley Publishing, Inc.

Information Nation: Seven Keys to Information Management Compliance, Second Edition

Published by
Wiley Publishing, Inc.
10475 Crosspoint Boulevard
Indianapolis, IN 46256
www.wiley.com

Copyright © 2009 by Randolph A. Kahn and Barclay T. Blair

Published by Wiley Publishing, Inc., Indianapolis, Indiana

Published simultaneously in Canada

ISBN: 978-0-470-45311-7

Manufactured in the United States of America

10 9 8 7 6 5 4 3 2 1

Library of Congress Cataloging-in-Publication Data:

Kahn, Randolph.

Information nation : seven keys to information management compliance / Randolph A. Kahn, ESQ., Barclay T. Blair. — 2nd ed.

p. cm.

Includes index.

ISBN 978-0-470-45311-7 (pbk.)

1. Management information systems—United States. 2. Information technology—United States—Management. 3. Business records—Data processing—Management. 4. Business records—Law and legislation—United States. 5. Disclosure of information—Law and legislation—United States. I. Blair, Barclay T. II. Title.

HD30.213.K34 2009

658.4'038—dc22

2008047044

For general information on our other products and services please contact our Customer Care Department within the United States at (877) 762-2974, outside the United States at (317) 572-3993 or fax (317) 572-4002.

To my amazing children, Dylan, Lily and Teddy,
who bring me life's greatest joy.
—*Randolph A. Kahn*

To Marianne and Jack
—*Barclay T. Blair*

About the Authors

Randolph A. Kahn is an internationally acclaimed speaker, consultant and award winning author of dozens of published works including *Privacy Nation, Information Nation Warrior, Information Nation: Seven Keys to Information Management Compliance*, and *E-Mail Rules*. Mr. Kahn was the recipient of the Britt Literary Award in 2004 for an article entitled "Records Management & Compliance: Making the Connection" and in 2005 for an article entitled "Stand and Deliver." He is an internationally recognized authority on the legal, compliance, and policy issues of information technology and information, and trusted advisor and consultant to Fortune 500 companies, governmental agencies and court systems.

As founder of Kahn Consulting, Inc., Mr. Kahn leads a team of information management, regulatory, compliance, and technology professionals who serve as consultants and advisors to major institutions around the globe. Each year Mr. Kahn speaks dozens of times around the globe to corporate and government institutions. Mr. Kahn can be contacted at 847-899-8487 or rkahn@KahnConsultingInc.com.

Barclay T. Blair is a consultant to Fortune 500 companies, software and hardware vendors, and government institutions, and is an author, speaker, and internationally recognized authority on a broad range of policy, compliance, and management issues related to information and information technology.

Barclay is the award-winning author of the books *Information Nation: Seven Keys to Information Management Compliance, Information Nation Warrior,* and *Privacy Nation*. Barclay has written and edited dozens of publications, speaks internationally on information management compliance issues, and has instructed at George Washington University. Barclay has edited and contributed to several books, including: *Email Rules; Secure Electronic Commerce;* and *Professional XML*. He can be contacted at 403-638-9302 or bblair@KillerAppsBlog.com.

Credits

Acknowledgments

The authors would like to thank AIIM International for their support in publishing the first edition of this book and other works of ours. We would also like to thank Andrew Cohen for his insightful contribution on GRC. Finally, thank you to W. Lawrence Wescott II for his valuable assistance in developing this second edition.

Contents

Introduction

Since the publication of the first edition of *Information Nation*, several significant developments have occurred that we believe warranted the publication of the second edition. The most important of these developments has been the electronic discovery amendments to the *Federal Rules of Civil Procedure*, which became effective on December 1, 2006. Many states have introduced, or are in the process of introducing, similar amendments to their rules of civil procedure.

These new rules have important implications for all organizations. Companies may find themselves at a severe disadvantage if they are not able to produce electronic documents in response to discovery requests under the new rules. The Seven Key approach introduced in the first edition provides a framework for firms to organize their information assets so that they can find responsive information to such requests. The second edition demonstrates specifically, via citations to the new Rules and case law decided under the new Rules, how firms incorporating an information management compliance philosophy into their corporate governance structure can succeed in this new environment.

The Seven Keys themselves have undergone some changes. Although consideration of the *Federal Sentencing Guidelines* by judges in their sentencing decisions is no longer mandatory (see discussion in Chapter 5), their importance for Information Management Compliance (IMC) remains unchanged.

IMC failures in companies can have spectacular consequences. The first edition highlighted the problems of Arthur Andersen in the Enron case. The second edition discusses a series of challenges facing Morgan Stanley (see Chapter 4). The most notable of these challenges occurred in the Coleman case, in which their continuing discovery of responsive electronic evidence (after certifying that all had been found) exasperated the judge and ultimately led to a nearly $1.6 billion jury verdict against the firm (although it was ultimately reversed on other grounds). Other compliance problems in different areas led to the imposition of significant fines by the SEC upon the firm.

The Morgan Stanley example again illustrates the consequences of information management compliance failure. The process of instituting an IMC culture is not accomplished overnight. The dedication and hard work required, however, pays off not only in the ability to respond to legal and regulatory requests but also in the ability to work more simply, more cheaply, and faster.

The second edition also incorporates the governance, risk and compliance (GRC) methodology. A summary of the methodology is provided by Andrew M. Cohen, Esq., Associate General Counsel for EMC Corporation (see Chapter 11). Although IMC is only a small subset of the overall GRC structure, GRC offers a toolset to help focus IMC efforts more effectively.

These developments are the reasons for the second edition of *Information Nation*. They demonstrate that it is even more important than ever to make the changes to your company to create a culture of Information Management Compliance.

Information Management Compliance

This is a book about changes in the Information Management landscape, resulting largely from cases like these and dozens of lower-profile cases. Most importantly, it is about how we can learn to avoid similar problems in our own organizations by developing and implementing Information Management Compliance programs that anticipate problems and take advantage of opportunities.

This is a book about approaching all types of Information Management activities with a new methodology, one that adopts the principles, controls, and discipline upon which many corporate compliance programs are built. While the world of records destruction is the starting point for our exploration, the book examines a broad range of Information Management activities that serve both legal and business needs, and are central to your organization's ongoing success.

This is a book about Information Management Compliance (IMC), which involves:

1. Developing Information Management criteria based on legal, regulatory, and business needs
2. Developing and implementing controls designed to ensure compliance with those policies and procedures

The first six chapters of this book define and explore the concepts of Information Management, Records Management, IMC, and the business and regulatory environments that we operate in today.

In the second part of the book we present the Seven Keys to Information Management Compliance—this is the practical, action-oriented part of the book. These Seven Keys are:

1. Good policies and procedures
2. Executive-level program responsibility
3. Proper delegation of program roles and components
4. Program dissemination, communication, and training
5. Auditing and monitoring to measure program compliance
6. Effective and consistent program enforcement
7. Continuous program improvement

As a model for these Seven Keys, we used a section of the *Federal Sentencing Guidelines* ("Guidelines").[1] The Guidelines are used by the federal courts to determine the appropriate punishment for individuals and organizations that violate the federal law. For many years, numerous companies have used the Guidelines to build general corporate compliance programs. However, until now, the Guidelines have generally been overlooked as a source of guidance for Information Management. The time has come to apply the compliance methodology outlined by the *Guidelines to Information Management*.

In this new era, Information Management requires a proactive approach that recognizes that legal protection *and* business value will result from taking a formal, disciplined, visible, funded, and sustained approach—an approach that begins with an understanding of how an organization's Information Management activities are likely to be judged by the courts, regulators, auditors, and its own executives and shareholders.

IMC is about more than making sure information is not destroyed because of the malicious or inadvertent acts of a few employees. Rather, it is a holistic approach that covers many areas of concern, including:

- Storage management
- Privacy
- Business continuity and disaster recovery planning
- Records Management
- Information security

- Transaction Management
- Application development and integration
- Technology purchasing and acquisition
- System configuration and management
- And many other areas

We wrote this book for a broad range of readers who have an interest in Information Management issues, with a specific focus on readers who have direct or indirect responsibility for making sure that information is properly used and managed in their organizations. The sphere of people who have some responsibility in this area seems to grow every day, now encompassing everyone from the CEO who needs to sign off on financial reports in accordance with Sarbanes-Oxley, to the IT professional wondering how backup tapes should be managed, to the compliance offer trying to ensure compliance with emerging privacy laws, to the administrative assistant just trying to decide what to do with all the email messages that his boss has asked him to print out and file, to the lawyer guiding the company through troubled legal waters.

Information Management encompasses management, administrative, operational, technological, human resources, Records Management, legal, and many other areas of an organization. The Seven Keys to IMC that we advance are designed to help professionals in each of these areas understand their responsibilities and what they must contribute to their organization's Information Management efforts.

Notes

[1] United States Sentencing Commission, *Guidelines Manual*, §3E1.1, Nov. 2002.

Laying the Foundations of Information Management Compliance

1

Why Information Management Matters

I n this first chapter, we will explore the concept of Information Management, how it has changed over time, and how it relates to other information-based activities across an organization. Understanding the essence of Information Management will lay the foundation for understanding Information Management Compliance (IMC).

Sink or Swim

In 2007, the digital universe (information created, captured, or replicated in digital form), was estimated to be 281 exabytes, or 281 billion gigabytes (GB).[1] For an estimated world population of 6.6 billion,[2] that is about 42.6 GB of data per person. About 210 billion e-mail messages are sent each day,[3] along with 32.2 billion instant messages.[4] The Radicati Group estimates that in 2008, a typical corporate e-mail account will send and receive about 18.5 MB of data per day. Forrester Research forecasts that the number of PCs worldwide will reach 2 billion by 2015. Exceptional growth is predicted in emerging markets, with a worldwide compound annual growth rate of more than 12 percent between 2003 and 2015.[5]

Information technology has become so commonplace in today's organizations that much of it is taken for granted. Some observers have even suggested that information technology and automation no longer offer "competitive advantage" because each competitor has essentially the same technology and level of automation.

From the largest Enterprise Resource Planning (ERP) application in use at a corporation with thousands of employees around the globe, to the tiny credit card–sized cell phone used by the independent consultant down the street, there are an ever-increasing number of software applications and hardware devices creating an ever-increasing amount of information. Information that must be sent, received, captured, accessed, stored, indexed, published, and so on. Put simply, information that must be managed.

The need for effective Information Management has never been greater.

What Is Information Management?

In the 1970s, the U.S. government commissioned a report that looked at the way government agencies were using information.[6] This report helped to popularize the concept of Information Management. The commission was concerned with both paper and electronic information and the way it was being managed through such diverse activities as library management, microforms, and word processing.

Over the ensuing decades, the term Information Management has come to be used in different ways by a number of groups, as the following definitions illustrate.

SELECTED DEFINITIONS OF INFORMATION MANAGEMENT

The application of management principles to the acquisition, organization, control, dissemination, and use of information relevant to the effective operation of organizations of all kinds.

"Information" here refers to all types of information of value, whether having their origin inside or outside the organization, including data resources, such as production data; records and files related, for example, to the personnel function; market research data; and competitive intelligence from a wide range of sources. Information management deals with the value, quality, ownership, use, and security of information in the context of organizational performance.

International Encyclopedia of Information and Library Science[7]

■

The proper organization and appropriate control of information transmitted by whatever means and including Records Management.

Comparative Glossary of Common Project Management Terms[8]

■

The administration, use, and transmission of information and the application of theories and techniques of information science to create, modify, or improve information-handling systems.

Environmental Protection Agency[9]

■

SELECTED DEFINITIONS OF INFORMATION MANAGEMENT
(Continued)

An imprecise term covering the various stages of information processing from production to storage and retrieval to dissemination towards the better working of an organisation; information can be from internal and external sources and in any format.

The Society for Information Management (UK)[10]

Changing Times, Changing Terms

As business practices and technologies have evolved, so too have the theories about Information Management. Like others working in fields where information technology had provided a radical transformative force, Information Management professionals and their industry groups have worked to stay ahead of the curve.

For example, AIIM International started life in 1943 as the National Microfilm Association, later became the Association for Information and Image Management, and today focuses on enterprise content management (ECM).[11] ECM is a vision of Information Management that refers to several related categories of information technology and processes including:

> *content/document management, business process management, enterprise portals, knowledge management, image management, data warehousing, and data mining.*[12]

ARMA International, an industry association for Information Management professionals, defines the activities of their members as "recorded information management (RIM),

> *a specialized field of information management that is concerned with the systematic analysis and control of operating records associated with business activities.*[13]

ARMA has also theorized that the future of RIM is SIM—Strategic Information Management,

> *that body of knowledge comprised of skills that will enable professionals and their organizations to make well-informed decisions resulting in a distinct competitive advantage in the business world. It draws upon skills from records and information management, information technology, and strategic management.*[14]

One of the most recent buzzwords in the Information Management world is *information lifecycle management* (ILM), which refers to the use of a combination of procedures and technology to managing an organization's information flow. Like many of the other terms used today, ILM is partly an old concept in a new wrapper, as the "lifecycle" approach to managing information has long been a central tenet of Records Management.

Part of the reason that terms like ILM, RIM, SIM, ECM, information resources management, and even Information Management have been adopted by these communities is a desire to escape the stigma perceived by some to be attached to the term Records Management (RM).

GRC is another new acronym, standing for Governance, Risk Management, and Compliance. Historically, these three activities have been viewed in isolation. The executive suite was responsible for the management, or governance of the enterprise. Risk management was viewed as a means for reducing insurance premiums. Compliance was an activity of the legal department; meant to keep the company from violating laws and regulations. GRC emphasizes the integration of these three activities into "an integrated framework ...with the purpose of providing a holistic view of a company's health and well-being."[15]

Outside the community of people and organizations responsible for managing records, Records Management is often perceived as a nonstrategic cost center. The average employee, or executive for that matter, commonly perceives RM simply as the basement where paper records are stored or part of the mailroom. It is easy to see why such perceptions have made it difficult for many RM departments to gain the visibility and funding they require to perform their corporate function. The relationship between Information Management and Records Management will be discussed further in a later chapter.

An Umbrella Term

Information Management is about determining which information created and received by your organization is valuable in some way, based on its content; making sure that this information is properly protected, stored, shared, and transmitted; and making it easily available to the people who need it, when they need it, and in a format that they can rely on.

Information Management, then, is an umbrella term that includes a variety of disciplines and activities, each focusing on different kinds of information and different kinds of management. In fact, in the broadest sense, Information Management touches on every business activity where information is received or created.

Table 1-1 provides some general examples of business activities related to Information Management. Although these activities have separate labels and definitions, in reality there is a great deal of overlap and interdependency among them.

THE PRICE OF FAILURE

The price of compliance failures can be huge in both financial and human terms. Failing to follow company policies because of laziness, lack of oversight, or negligence can and does have profound consequences.

For example, in *Murphy Oil USA, Inc. v. Fluor Daniel, Inc,*[16] the court heard a dispute in which Murphy Oil wanted Fluor Daniel to go through nearly 20 million pages of e-mail records to see if any of those records related to the case. The reason that there were so many pages of e-mail to search through is that Fluor had apparently not been following its own policy, as the court noted:

"Fluor's email retention policy provided that backup tapes were recycled after 45 days. If Fluor had followed this policy, the email issue would be moot. Fluor does not explain why, but it maintained its backup tapes for the entire 14-month period."

Fluor estimated that the cost of providing the 20 million pages of e-mail and attachments would be in excess of $6 million, and would take six months—far more than the cost would have been if they had followed their own policy.

Cases like these illustrate the need for organizations to develop an accurate estimate of the Total Cost of Failure (TCF) of Information Management failures. See Chapter 12 for more information on calculating the price of Information Management failures.

Table 1-1: Business Activities Related to Information Management

Activity	Kinds of Information	Basic Goal
Records management	Business records	Making sure that business records are properly retained for legal, compliance, and business purposes, and properly disposed of when no longer needed
Document management	"Documents"—a wide range of digital information	Ensuring that there are controls in place for the creation and storage of business documents so that they are easily accessible to knowledge workers and others
Knowledge management	Operational information of all kinds	Ensuring that the knowledge of some individuals and groups in an organization is harnessed for use by others in the organization
Enterprise content management	Umbrella term for technologies, tools, and methods used to capture, manage, store, preserve, and deliver content across an enterprise	Often used as a broad term to include activities such as document management, knowledge management, and published content (including website content)
Information security	All valuable information, with a focus on sensitive, confidential, and proprietary info	Ensuring that valuable information is accessible only to those authorized to see it, and ensuring its trustworthiness
Information privacy	Sensitive information, as determined by policy or law, including information about clients, customers, and patients	Ensuring that the collection of and access to sensitive information is properly controlled
Disaster recovery	Information needed to continue business operations	Ensuring that vital information required to operate the business can be recovered in a timely fashion after a disaster
Customer/ client relationship management	Information about an organization's interactions with customers/clients and prospects	Ensuring that the customers' experience with a company is satisfactory and consistent; identifying customer patterns that can lead to more revenue
Storage management	All stored digital business information	Ensuring that storage resources such as disk drives and backup media are used cost-effectively
Data mining	Structured information, such as databases	Providing tools and techniques for collecting and analyzing stored data

Determine Your Needs

Information Management encompasses many different activities, disciplines, people, and—no doubt—departments in your organization. The people responsible for operating the company firewall, for example, are probably in a different part of the building from the people who figure out how the customer relationship management system should work. This is part of the challenge inherent to Information Management—it is difficult to get an overall picture of how your company manages its information.

When examining your Information Management needs, start by getting the "10,000-foot view," and then work down into the details. This will require executive involvement, as we'll explore in Key 2. It will also require research into the activities of various departments throughout your organization.

Make a list of all the activities in your organization that fall under the Information Management umbrella. Since many of these activities center on technology, your IT/IS department may be a good place to start.

For example, find out the following:

- Who is responsible for each Information Management activity on your list? Does responsibility reside with a Records Management department, a compliance department, the IT/IS department, or a combination of these and others?
- Are there policies and practices that govern each activity? For example, do employees know if they can use the company e-mail system for personal business, and does the webmaster know what kinds of content needs to be approved by the general counsel before being posted on the company website?
- Does your organization use a different term for Information Management that means the same thing? If so, ensure that the term is well understood throughout the company and used consistently.
- Is the Records Management expertise in your company being applied to information technology? In other words, do the Records Management people and the IT people coordinate their activities?
- When was the last time that policies were reviewed to make sure that they have kept pace with new laws and regulations that affect your industry? If you haven't reviewed your policies since 2001, for example, you should do so to ensure compliance with the Sarbanes-Oxley Act of 2002.

Answering these questions will help your organization to develop a consistent approach to Records and Information Management.

Notes

[1] "The Diverse and Exploding Digital Universe," IDC White Paper, 2008.

[2] Population Reference Bureau, 2007 World Population Data Sheet.

[3] Yuki Noguchi, "Make It Stop! Crushed by Too Many E-Mails," npr.com, 6/16/2008, http://www.npr.org/templates/story/story.php?storyId=91366853.

[4] Alex Moskalyuk, zdnet.com, http://blogs.zdnet.com/ITFacts/?p=8425

[5] Siobhan Chapman, "PC Numbers set to hit 1 billion," Computerworld UK, June 12, 2007.

[6] National Commission on Federal Paperwork in 1977.

[7] "Information Management," International Encyclopedia of Information and Library Science, 2nd ed. Edited by John Feather and Paul Sturges. London: Routledge, 2002.

[8] Wideman, R. Max, Wideman, Comparative Glossary of Common Project Management Terms v3.1, March 2002.

[9] U.S. Environmental Protection Agency glossary. Online at http://www.epa.gov/records/gloss/gloss05.htm

[10] Aslib, The Association for Information Management glossary. Online at http://www.aslib.com/info/glossary.html

[11] AIIM International, "About AIIM." Online at http://www.aiim.org/article_aiim.asp?ID=18274

[12] Ibid.

[13] ARMA International, "Information Management: A Business Imperative: FAQs for Corporate Executives and Decision Makers," 2002.

[14] ARMA International, "Is Strategic Information Management Your Destiny?" October 2000. Online at http://www.arma.org/about/sim_faq.cfm

[15] Linda Musthaler and Brian Musthaler, "Governance, risk management and compliance, and what it means to you," Network World, May 7, 2007.

[16] Murphy Oil USA, Inc. v. Fluor Daniel, Inc., 2002 U.S. Dist. LEXIS 3196 (U.S. Dist., 2002).

2

Building the Foundation: Defining Records

Organizations must have a consistent method for determining if information is a record and therefore needs to be retained and managed according to special rules. Determining this can be complex, but as this chapter explores, there are several guidelines that organizations can use to help.

Determining If Information Is a Record

An organization does not have to retain all information that it creates or receives. However, internal policies, laws, regulations, standards, and best practices dictate that certain kinds of information—namely, records—be retained and managed in a specific way. Thus, it is obviously important that organizations have a method for identifying records.

In the digital world, there are many kinds of electronic documents, messages, notes, and various other kinds of digital files and other "stuff" that might or might not be considered a record. If all of this incredible volume of digital stuff had to be captured and managed, most businesses would be overwhelmed or even crushed beneath its weight. However, to make it even more difficult, getting rid of the wrong information can have severe legal consequences.

It quickly becomes apparent that an organization needs a way to determine which information it should retain as a record and which information can be discarded. In order to do this, organizations must first define and understand the function of records.

> QUIZ TIME:
> WHICH DIGITAL INFORMATION MIGHT NEED TO BE RETAINED?
>
> - "Clicks" on your company's Web page regarding customer purchases?
> - Mass voicemail messages to customers about a new product offering?
> - Employee 401(k) plan selections made via a telephone keypad on your company's Interactive Voice Response (IVR) telephone system?
> - Voicemail from a regulator asking questions about a mandatory filing?
> - An instant message from a business partner agreeing to pay half the marketing costs of a new product initiative?
>
> If you answered yes to all of the above, you are correct. The fact that the above information exists in digital form, and may appear more casual or ephemeral than information in paper or other form, does not diminish your organization's obligation to retain information that has business, operational, legal, regulatory, and/or historical significance.

Defining Records

The term *record* has been defined in a number of ways by different communities involved in Records Management. It is important that your organization adopt a definition that can be supported by your Records Management program.

Although each of these definitions takes a different approach to defining the term *record*, there is also a great deal of commonality here. Each emphasizes the idea that a record must actually be *recorded* in some way, whether as a "writing" as described by the law dictionary, or as "machine readable materials" as described in the definition used by the NARA. Similarly, the definitions make clear that the purpose of a record is to serve as evidence of something, such as a "court proceeding" in the case of the Black's definition, or "the transaction of business," as defined by ISO.

SELECTED DEFINITIONS OF RECORD

A written account of some act, court proceeding, transaction, or instrument, drawn up, under authority of law, by proper officer, and designed to remain as a memorial or permanent evidence of the matters to which it relates.
   Black's Law Dictionary

■

Information created, received and maintained as evidence and information by an organization, or person, in pursuance of legal obligations or in the transaction of business.
   International Organization for Standardization (ISO)[1]

■

All books, papers, maps, photographs, machine readable materials, or other documentary materials, regardless of physical form or characteristics, made or received by an agency of the United States Government under Federal law or in connection with the transaction of public business and preserved or appropriate for preservation by that agency or its legitimate successor as evidence of the organization, functions, policies, decisions, procedures, operations, or other activities of the Government or because of the informational value of data in them. Library and museum material made or acquired and preserved solely for reference or exhibition purposes, extra copies of documents preserved only for convenience of reference, and stocks of publications and of processed documents are not included.
   U.S. federal law (44 U.S.C. 3301), the definition also used by the U.S. National Archives and Records Administration, or NARA

It is instructive to note that the more recently created (in the case of the ISO definition) and specific (in the case of the federal government definition) definitions make clear that records serve both a legal *and* a business purpose. The focus on records as *business* evidence represents an ongoing shift that has been occurring in the Information Management world for some time, as organizations have come to realize how fundamental information has become to their operations. After all, in the "information age," where capturing, managing, and using information has become a central business activity in most large organizations, the business purpose of records and other information is self-evident.

Why These Definitions Matter

Recently in our consulting practice, while performing a final review of e-mail retention guidelines we had drafted for a client, we noticed that the definition of "record" had been changed by our client, who had added the following statement to the draft:

> *A Record is inscribed on a tangible medium and, as such, is retrievable in a viewable form.*

We reminded the client's attorney that there were in fact many records in use at their company that did not fit the new definition. These included interactive voice response records, audiotapes of meetings, and other records that are indeed "inscribed on a tangible medium," but are not "retrievable in viewable form." The definition needed to be changed.

There is currently no definition of "record" that is universally used by all organizations, and for good reason. Definitions serve the community that they are created by, and each community has different needs. There is no reason why your organization's definition of "record" needs to strictly conform to other organizations in your industry. However, it only makes sense to leverage the work that organizations such as ISO, for example, have done when defining records. The key characteristic of a good definition for your purposes is that it is broad enough to encompass all the information you need to retain for business, operational, legal, regulatory, and/or historical purposes, without being so broad that employees cannot understand or apply it in practice.

Our definition of "record" below is the one that we often use in our consulting practice, and encompasses key records concepts:

> *A record is information recorded on a tangible medium (paper and electronic media being two common examples) and intentionally retained and managed as evidence of an organization's activities, events, or transactions for business, operational, legal, regulatory, and/or historical purposes.*

See Chapter 3 for an example of the business, operational, and regulatory purposes that records fulfill.

DEFINING "BUSINESS INFORMATION"

When drafting policies and discussing Information Management issues, there are many occasions where it is necessary to broadly refer to all information related to an organization's business operations, whether or not that information qualifies as a record and is retained and managed according to record retention rules. This is necessary, for example, when discussing ownership of information assets in Information Management policies (see Chapter 3 for more information).

Many organizations use the term "business information." Our baseline definition for "business information," which we customize according to the type of client, is:

Information generated or received by the company or its employees and used in the operation of our business. Business information includes records, data, and documents stored in any form (e.g., paper, electronic, audio and video recordings, and imaging media).

Why We Retain Records

Records are central to every organization's ability to operate its business. Without a consistent way to identify and manage records, and to properly dispose of unneeded information, the following functions of records will be threatened:

- To serve customers (e.g., by providing timely access to accurate purchasing info)
- To plan and forecast (e.g., by consulting records of past sales performance)
- To serve as an "organizational memory" (e.g., corporate archives and libraries)
- To meet legal obligations (e.g., tax laws)
- To protect legal and business interests (e.g., contracts)
- To comply with regulations (e.g., health, safety, and environmental laws)
- To satisfy the courts (e.g., retaining records subject to subpoena)
- To help resolve disagreements and disputes (e.g., regarding agreements, promises, claims, or representations)

The ability to properly and consistently retain business records is especially important today, as more and more records are in electronic form—a form that makes it much easier to lose, alter, disseminate, replicate, or improperly dispose of records (a topic explored in detail throughout this book).

IS IT "JUST DATA," OR IS IT A RECORD?

Too many organizations make the mistake of viewing the output of IT systems, the contents of databases, data streams, and other electronic information as "just data" that has limited value to their organizations. However, before being so quick to pass judgment on this digital information, ask yourself the following questions—that "data" may be more important than you think:

- Does it document a business activity?
- Does the information have business, operational, legal, regulatory, and/or historic value to the company?
- If it were in paper form, would it be retained?
- Does the law expect that your organization will retain it?
- Could it help resolve a dispute in the future?

Not All Information Has to Be Retained

It is, of course, not wrongful for a manager to instruct his employees to comply with a valid document retention policy under ordinary circumstances.

> *Where an organization…keeps the relevant records for the time period mandated by law, without additional evidence of wrongdoing that should have put management on notice…, there is nothing to warrant a finding of spoliation.*
>
> United States v. Kitsap Physicians Serv.[3]

As the preceding quote demonstrates, the courts have made clear that organizations do not have to retain all the information that they create or receive, nor do they have to retain all records indefinitely. In fact, a key benefit of developing a consistent method for identifying and managing records is that it allows organizations to get rid of unneeded information and records without fear of legal sanctions. This has the additional benefit of reducing the burden on precious enterprise storage resources that are already under the strain of volumes of e-mail messages, instant messages, documents, spreadsheets, and so on.

Disposition of unneeded information also enhances a company's GRC posture. There is less information to manage, a lower likelihood that a document "time bomb" is lurking within the archives, and a smaller compliance burden.

Top 10 Reasons *Not* to Keep Everything Forever

Organizations are not required too keep all information forever. In fact, there are several reasons why organizations should ensure that they dispose of unnecessary information:

1. The law does not require it.
2. Only increases the risk of outdated documents being exposed that can damage the company's legal position.
3. May require maintenance of expensive "legacy" software and hardware to recreate original content years after it was created.
4. Aged storage media needs to be refreshed and data migrated to ensure continued access—an expensive and time-consuming process.
5. Data tends to grow exponentially, making it increasingly difficult to retrieve what you are looking for.
6. Costs associated with discovery in litigation increase with the volume of data that must be reviewed.
7. Purchasing, managing, maintaining, and migrating excess storage media is expensive.
8. Many business processes, from serving customers to forecasting sales, are slower and less effective when systems are bogged down with useless information.
9. Makes it harder to respond quickly to regulators and courts, either of which can dictate fast turnaround times for providing specific information.
10. Makes it impractical and cost-prohibitive to apply controls and technology to information that requires special handling, such as private customer data.

Medium Does Not Matter

Imagine that you receive the following memo:

> *ATTN: All Employees*
>
> *RE: Corporate Efficiency*
>
> *The Executive Records Management Committee has decided that in order to save money and cut down on office clutter, we will be destroying all files that reside in gray filing cabinets. Consequently, we request that all employees IMMEDIATELY remove all files in gray filing cabinets in their vicinity and place them in industrial shredders that will be provided.*
>
> *Only gray filing cabinets are affected by this directive. Blue and tan filing cabinets are exempt. Thank your for your cooperation.*
>
> Executive Records Management Committee

The thinking behind such a memo would be mystifying. How could the company get away with destroying files without any regard to their content, just because they reside in gray filing cabinets?

This obviously would never happen in the paper world, but it happens all the time in the digital world. Organizations routinely purge their enterprise e-mail systems every 30, 60, or 90 days without regard for the value of the information that is contained in those purged e-mail messages. Not only does this approach eliminate the potential benefits of harnessing the knowledge that is captured in the e-mail system, but the company may also open itself up to serious legal consequences as a result of this practice.

How can the company assume that the e-mail system does not contain records simply because the medium is e-mail? Indiscriminately purging an entire e-mail system after a short period of time and without regard to the content is just like indiscriminately purging paper files that that are housed in gray filing cabinets.

The lesson here is that the medium does not matter when deciding whether or not information qualifies as a record. E-mail systems, text messaging services, voicemail systems, and peer-to-peer networks are all just transmission vehicles for information that may or may not be a record. In other words, the method used to send, create, or receive information, and the medium used to store information, do not matter when determining if certain content qualifies as a record. The laws usually do not differentiate when it comes to medium, and neither should your organization.

Intent Does Matter

Our definition of a record presented earlier states that a record is "intentionally retained and managed as evidence of an organization's activities, events, or transactions."

Intent provides a key to determining if a specific piece of information is in fact a record. Although this can be challenging in the paper world, it is even harder in the digital world, where multiple copies of an e-mail message and its attachments can exist on several computers around the globe at the same time. Assuming a particular e-mail message qualifies as a business record, which copy (or copies) of the e-mail must be retained and managed?

Let's look at a case where a word processing document is passed amongst several colleagues via e-mail, each person adding comments and revisions along the way. Each employee has now saved several copies and versions of the document in his or her file system, and all those versions are saved on the central e-mail server.

Which copy of this document should be retained as the record? If the company's Records Management policy states that only the final version of this type of document must be captured and retained in a central Records Management system, then the final version of the document is the record, and all other copies can be safely deleted, barring any law or regulation to the contrary.[4]

In other words, the company has made clear, through its policy and actions, that the final version is intended to be the "official" record. Intent is the key.

Intent is critical because digital information has qualities that can make it difficult to determine which copy of a file is the official record. These qualities include:

- The ability to make infinite perfect copies of an electronic file
- The ease of instantly disseminating perfect copies to people around the globe at the touch of key
- The difficulty of tracking versions of the same file without special software
- The ease of altering a digital file, both inadvertently and intentionally

In general, only the "official" version of a record needs to be retained and managed.

Determining which copy of a digital file is the official record is important for a variety of reasons. First, barring any legal reason to the contrary, it allows organizations to retain a single copy of a file and discard the rest with legal comfort, resulting in storage cost savings. Second, it reduces the chance that courts will make an organization search through gigabytes of data for all copies of a file in the course of discovery in a trial or investigation (more on this later). Third, it makes it easier for employees to properly retain records of their work.

Let's look at another example involving a file disseminated by e-mail among colleagues. If you send an important e-mail message (which qualifies as a record) to Tom, and send copies (using the cc: address field) to Dick and Harry as well, now there are four copies of the e-mail message in existence (plus copies on the central e-mail server). Is one of them an official record that must be retained and managed?

Different organizations might answer this question differently. As a matter of policy, many would say that only Tom (the person to whom the e-mail was sent directly), and not Dick or Harry (the cc'd parties), needs to retain a copy of the e-mail for recordkeeping purposes. So, the direct recipient's copy of the e-mail would be the only official record, as it is the one retained for recordkeeping purposes; the other copies can be disposed of because an official record has been designated and retained.

However, there are many subtleties to this issue. Some organizations may only require the sender to retain the message, while others may require anyone who is required to take action as a result of the e-mail message, regardless of whether or not they are the direct recipient to retain a copy. The right answer for your organization derives from a combination of its organizational culture, technical capabilities, regulatory environment, and litigation history.

What is certain is that all organizations must ensure that procedures for designating and retaining "official records" are formally documented, widely disseminated, and properly understood and enforced—as with any other Information Management policy or procedure. Doing so establishes your organization's intent to capture, retain, and manage specific copies or versions of records as official records. Formally establishing this intent reduces the likelihood that a court, regulator, auditor, or other outside party will take issue with the disposition of non-official records.

THE BUSINESS RECORDS EXCEPTION TO THE HEARSAY RULE

When the courts consider evidence in a case, they typically prefer to have testimony from individuals who have direct, first-hand knowledge of the matter at hand—for example, an eyewitness, a party to the conversation in question, or someone involved in the creation of a document or record. This type of testimony is generally thought most likely to be trustworthy and accurate. In most cases, non-direct, second-hand testimony is considered to be "hearsay" and cannot be admitted as evidence.

Business records are considered to be a form of hearsay but are generally allowable under the "business records" exception to the hearsay rule. This exception is described in the Federal Rules of Evidence (FRE), a set of rules for how evidence is handled in federal courts. Among other things, the FRE require that the business records must have been "kept in the course of a regularly conducted business," and "the source of information or the method or circumstances of preparation" must be trustworthy.[5]

Record Qualification Checklist

Here is a checklist to help you apply the definition of a record to the information within your organization. This list is not exhaustive, but represents a sampling of criteria.

It is probably a record if:

- A regulation or statute says it must be retained.
- It contains valuable information about business operations.
- It contains information that must be filed with a regulator.
- It is an instant message that was used to negotiate a contract.
- It is a voicemail message from a regulator about official business.
- The sales forecast depends on information it contains.
- It is the final version of a contract.
- It has business, compliance, historical, operational, and/or legal value or significance to the organization.

Survey: Employee Responsibility for Records and Information

The following survey will help you understand employee responsibility for *records* and *information*.

1. Does the company provide employees with retention rules for electronic records?
2. Does the company provide guidance and training for all employees on what information can be sent across the Internet?
3. Do all employees receive training on their Records Management responsibilities as part of their new employee orientation?
4. Does the company provide specific rules about how and where to retain e-mail records that require long-term retention?
5. Are employees provided with any technological solutions or tools to secure laptops, PDAs, or other handheld computers?

If you answered "No" to any of the above, your organization likely has more work to do to get the employees engaged in helping manage its information assets.

Notes

[1] ISO 15489-11 - Information and documentation—Records Management—Part 1: General / ISO, Geneva, 2001.

[2] *Andersen v. U.S.*, 544 U.S. 696, 704 (2005).

[3] *U.S. v. Kitsap Physicians Serv.*, 314 F.3d 995, 1001-02 (9th cir. 2002).

[4] It should be noted that this is only an example, and there may in fact be cases where an organization is obligated to keep all drafts and revisions of a document in order to comply with law or regulation.

[5] *Federal Rules of Evidence* 803(6).

3

An Overview of Records Management

In Chapter 1, we explored how diverse Information Management activities fit together. In Chapter 2, we defined the term *record* and examined the need for organizations to properly identify and retain business records. In this chapter we will look in detail at the systematic management of records (i.e., Records Management) and examine how Records Management and Information Management fit together.

Defining Records Management

Information Management is a broad category of activities, all of which must be carried out with a view to compliance. For example, it is just as important that an organization's information security policies reflect current laws as it is for a customer relationship management application to protect customer privacy. Both areas are part of Information Management, and both must be compliant with relevant criteria.

In many ways, however, Records Management is not just another activity under the umbrella of Information Management. In fact, Records Management typically deals with the most sensitive, valuable, and challenging information in an organization. This is why we have chosen to devote an entire chapter to the topic.

Whereas Information Management is a broad activity encompassing many different types of information and management activities, Records Management focuses on a particular type of information, namely records. In this sense, Records Management is a subset or component of Information Management. Records Management is a complex topic, and the purpose of this chapter is not to provide an exhaustive overview of it, but rather to highlight key issues that relate to Information Management Compliance (IMC).

As the definitions that follow demonstrate, there are many different takes on Records Management. However, each of the definitions makes clear that Records Management is focused on the formal and systematic management of important information from the time it is "born" to the time it no longer serves a purpose within an organization and is disposed of.

SELECTED DEFINITIONS OF RECORDS MANAGEMENT

Field of management responsible for the efficient and systematic control of the creation, receipt, maintenance, use and disposition of records, including processes for capturing and maintaining evidence of and information about business activities and transactions in the form of records.
   ISO[1]

■

From the Federal perspective, it is the planning, controlling, directing, organizing, training, promoting, and other managerial activities involved in records creation, maintenance and use, and disposition in order to achieve adequate and proper documentation of the policies and transactions of the Federal Government (36 CFR 1220.14).
   NARA (U.S. National Archives and Records Administration)[2]

■

The planning, controlling, directing, organizing, training, promoting, and other managerial activities involving the lifecycle of information, including creation, maintenance (use, storage, retrieval), and disposal, regardless of media.
   U.S. Department of Defense[3]

The Lifecycle Approach

Contemporary Records Management is largely based on what is commonly known as a *lifecycle*. Information is viewed as having a lifecycle with a beginning, middle, and end—much like any living organism. However, a record's lifecycle isn't so much natural as it is imposed through a Records Management program. Borrowing from the U.S. Department of Defense definition above, we can say that this lifecycle goes through the following stages:

1. Creation
2. Use
3. Storage
4. Retrieval
5. Disposal

There are other ways to break down the various stages in the lifecycle, but put simply, the lifecycle includes everything that happens to a record from the time it is created until the time it is disposed of.

Information Assets

The lifecycle approach is valuable because it enables organizations to perceive business records as assets with value that changes over time—just like any other asset. That is why records and other business information are often referred to as *information assets*.

Take, for example, a potential customer submitting a request for information about a new drug through a form on a pharmaceutical company's website. In this example, the information contained in the customer request serves several purposes throughout its lifecycle, especially these three:

1. **Business purpose.** First, the information in the customer's request is required simply for the purposes of responding appropriately. The request details what the customer wants and enables the company representative to craft a useful response. In this sense, the record serves a clear business purpose. If the request were somehow lost, altered, or disposed of before the representative could generate a response, then a potential business opportunity would be lost.

2. **Operational purpose.** Once the customer has been satisfied, there may be many operational purposes for the information. For example, the company could keep track of how many customers have requested information in order to gauge the success of marketing programs. Or the company could keep track of how many times customers ask the same

questions, and if justified, create a simple FAQ, automated response, or perhaps a more detailed, searchable knowledge base about this particular product, as many companies do. In these examples, the objective at this stage in the information lifecycle is to provide information that can be used for business planning, customer relationship management, and other operational purposes.

3. **Regulatory purposes.** Depending on the nature of the information request, the pharmaceutical company may have an obligation to retain a record of the customer exchange, according to Food and Drug Administration regulations. In this case, managing the record helps the company comply with the law and protects it from other legal problems that may arise.

This simple example demonstrates some of the roles that records play throughout their lifecycle. Although the purpose of the records and the source of its value may change over time, the need to properly retain and manage the record does not.

Components of a Records Management Program

The makeup of Records Management programs varies from organization to organization, according to size, the nature of the company's business activities, organizational culture, regulatory environment, and several other factors. Records Management programs range from very formal, broad programs with dedicated departments and dozens of employees, to informal programs that are run by an administrator on an ad hoc basis.

Despite this variability, there are several fundamental components that every Records Management program should consist of to be adequate, effective, and efficient.

The U.S. Environmental Protection Agency (EPA) definition of a Records Management program provides a useful overview of its basic elements.

According to the EPA, a Records Management program is:

A planned, coordinated set of policies, procedures, and activities needed to manage an agency's recorded information. Encompasses

the creation, maintenance and use, and disposition of records,
regardless of media. Essential elements include issuing up-to-date
program directives, properly training those responsible for implemen-
tation, publicizing the program, and carefully evaluating the results
to ensure adequacy, effectiveness, and efficiency.[4]

By breaking this definition down and paraphrasing it, we can identify the critical elements of a Records Management program.

A Records Management program is a planned, coordinated set of policies, procedures, and activities designed to manage recorded information through its lifecycle, regardless of the media upon which it is recorded. Essential elements include:

- Up-to-date program directives
- Proper training to ensure thorough implementation
- Building organizational awareness of the program
- Auditing the program for adequacy, effectiveness, and efficiency

Additional components of successful Records Management programs are listed here and are explored in greater detail throughout the book:

- A comprehensive body of policies, procedures, and implementation guidelines dealing with issues of record creation, what to retain, where, by whom, classification, ownership of records, security, disposition, and so on
- Completion of a records inventory and other information gathering to determine what records are in use and the reason for their use so that laws and regulations can be consulted about periods of retention
- Retention rules (based on legal requirements, legal considerations, and business needs) that tell employees how long to retain various categories of records
- A Records Management organization with sufficient support, visibility, accountability, budget, and staff to fulfill the goals of the Records Management program
- A formal process (often called a *Records or Legal Hold* process for finding, preserving, and producing records and other tangible evidence in

the context of expected or current litigation, audits, investigations, and other formal proceedings

- A comprehensive training program for all employees to ensure that they understand their Records Management responsibilities and how to fulfill them

- Special rules for managing and retaining e-mail and other types of electronic records, as required

- Special rules for handling special records, such as Vital, Privileged, Trade Secret, and Private records

- An auditing or review mechanism to ensure that employees are doing what they are supposed to regarding the management of records

Managing Electronic Records

Electronic records (e-records) can be used in place of paper records for more purposes and in more jurisdictions than ever before. E-records can also be offered as evidence in most jurisdictions without concern that they will be deemed "inadmissible" merely because they are not in paper form, or because they are not "an original." The federal E-SIGN Act, for example, clarifies that "a signature, contract, or other record...may not be denied legal effect, validity, or enforceability solely because it is in electronic form."[5] Cases such as *U.S. v. Catabran* make clear that "it is immaterial that the business record is maintained in a computer rather than in company books," for the purposes of admissibility.[6]

Laws regarding electronic information and records generally address what is acceptable to the courts, what is acceptable to regulators and government agencies, or both. At the same time, these laws and regulations typically take the approach of either allowing the use of electronic information for legal and regulatory purposes, or of stipulating specific requirements designed to ensure that electronic records and evidence are trustworthy, complete, reliable, secure, and so on. Laws and regulations, even those that provide specific criteria, tend to be technology-neutral. That is, they do not require the use of a particular technology.

Electronic Records Must Be Trustworthy

At the same time, organizations need to be aware that because electronic records and information can be relied upon in more situations than ever before, courts and regulators expect electronic records to be trustworthy.

Trustworthy records are the product of informed and committed efforts to properly manage them. Building good electronic records begins with an understanding of what makes them trustworthy.

Trustworthiness is most accurately thought of as a quality that results from the sum total of the people, procedures, environments, strategies, and technologies used throughout the lifecycle of a business record. Trustworthiness suggests that a court, regulator, or auditor—and the organization itself—can trust and rely upon the content of a record. Trustworthiness of electronic records is a key component in the GRC matrix. Assessment of trustworthiness of electronic records must be a strong consideration in the strategic risk-based allocation of resources—compliance risks will rise, and management cannot rely on the integrity of the information upon which decisions are based, if data is not trustworthy.

A trustworthy electronic record has four key qualities, including:

1. **Integrity.** An e-record has integrity if it can be demonstrated that its contents have not been altered since the e-record was created, and that the record remained complete from its creation to disposition.

2. **Accuracy.** An e-record is accurate if it contains the information it is supposed to contain, as originally intended, and the content remains the same over its entire lifecycle.

3. **Authenticity.** An e-record is said to be authentic if it is in fact "what it purports to be." That is, the source or origin of the e-record can be reliably demonstrated. This often requires proof of who generated an e-record, and who controlled it over its lifecycle (often called an *audit trail*).

4. **Accessibility.** Trustworthiness implies that an organization or an outside party will be able to rely on an e-record for business, legal, or compliance purposes. A record that cannot be accessed in a timely fashion during its lifecycle precludes its use for these purposes. Accessibility can be threatened by poor indexing, the finite life span of storage media, hardware

obsolescence, software incompatibility, environmental degradation, and many other factors.

Digital Trustworthiness Is a Challenge

Regulators demand that standards of information integrity and accuracy must be met. The courts have excluded electronic evidence that they have deemed untrustworthy. In addition, it does an organization little good to expend the resources necessary to manage e-records if the organization itself cannot be sure of their integrity. Therefore, the issue of trustworthiness is more than just a legal issue—it is central to an organization's ability to plan, strategize, and operate its business.

While the issue of trustworthiness may seem self-explanatory when dealing with paper records, e-records have several unique characteristics that make their management challenging. These qualities include:

1. **Complexity.** Understanding the creation of a paper record is usually straightforward. Many e-records, however, are created using complex technological processes that may be hard to explain to a court or regulator, which can add to the time and expense of presenting complex electronic evidence.
2. **Portability.** E-records can be easily created and distributed, which can make it more difficult to track their origin and use throughout their life span.
3. **Alterability.** Unlike the physical bond of ink on paper, most e-records provide no such inherent characteristics that prevent their inadvertent or deliberate alteration—even though certain storage technologies can prohibit unauthorized alteration or deletion.
4. **Hardware and software.** E-records rely on hardware and software for their display and use—hardware and software that may not always be available.
5. **Multiple parts.** Paper records contain all of their information within the "four corners" of a document. E-records, on the other hand, can contain metadata and exist in multiple parts in multiple locations—thus making their capture, retrieval, and presentation problematic.

EXCLUDING ELECTRONIC EVIDENCE

The courts can and will exclude (or minimize the evidentiary value of) unauthenticated evidence or evidence that is otherwise deemed to be untrustworthy, as the selection of cases below demonstrates:

> *Monotype v. International Typeface*—e-mail evidence supporting the defendant's case was excluded.[7]
> *Pettiford v. N.C HHS*—the plaintiff's failure to properly authenticate e-mail messages offered as evidence resulted in the court refusing to consider them as evidence, even though they supported her claim.[8]
> *Sea-Land Serv. v. Lozen Int'l*—unauthenticated electronic evidence was also excluded.[9]
> *Gamber-Johnson v. Trans Data Net Corp*—the court excluded evidence regarding a contractual dispute, which contributed to the court awarding damages for breach of contract to the plaintiff.[10]

There have been many more cases where electronic evidence was excluded, or its persuasiveness in the courtroom was diminished, because the evidence could not be adequately authenticated.

Technology Can Help with Trustworthiness

Although laws and regulations regarding electronic records and digital information are generally technology-neutral, many of these laws and regulations also recognize that the functionality and configuration of software and hardware plays a large role in digital trustworthiness. While these laws and regulations may not describe a specific kind of technology, they do specify functional criteria that must be met by technology used in the management, storage, and retention of required records. These laws and regulations recognize that not all technology is created equal when it comes to ensuring the trustworthiness of electronic records. It is important that your organization also recognizes this fact when selecting and implementing technology for storing and managing electronic records.

One of the clearest examples of this type of regulation is 17 CFR § 240.17a-4, a rule promulgated by the SEC addressing records retention and management requirements for broker-dealers. Since 1997, 17a-4 has allowed broker-dealers to retain required records in electronic form, provided that certain requirements are met.

One of these requirements is that the electronic storage media used "[p]reserve the records exclusively in a non-rewriteable, non-erasable format."[11] The SEC has stated that this requirement "is designed to ensure that electronic records are capable of being accurately reproduced for later reference by maintaining the records in unalterable form."[12]

The SEC has clarified that a number of storage technologies and techniques may be used to fulfill this requirement of the regulation, including storage media (such as certain kinds of optical discs and magnetic tape) that offers write-once, read-many (WORM) functionality, or "an electronic storage system that prevents the overwriting, erasing, or otherwise altering of a record during its required retention period through the use of integrated hardware and software control codes."[13]

The key element of the storage system used to comply with the regulation is that it must protect the integrity, accuracy, authenticity, and accessibility of electronic records—the four elements of electronic record trustworthiness outlined above.

Proper technology selection and implementation is important in all facets of IMC, from protecting privacy through encryption and database security, to building intranet-based applications in a way that enables trustworthy records to be captured and retained. This concept is explored in more detail throughout the book.

Notes

[1] ISO 15489, Information and documentation—Records management, October 2001.

[2] NARA, "Context for Electronic Records Management." Online at
   `http://www.archives.gov/records_management/policy_and_guidance/`
   `baseline_organizational_information_survey.html`

[3] DoD 5015.2-STD, June 19, 2002.

[4] U.S. Environmental Protection Agency glossary. Online at `http://www.epa.gov/records/gloss/gloss05.htm`

[5] Public Law 106-229, Section 101(a)(1).

[6] *United States v. Catabran*, 836 F.2d 453, 457 (9th Cir. 1988).

[7] *Monotype Corp. PLC v. International Typeface Corp.*, 43 F.3d 443.

[8] *Pettiford v. N.C. HHS*, 2002 U.S. Dist. LEXIS 18879.

[9] *Sea-Land Serv. v. Lozen Int'l, LLC*, 285 F.3d 808.

[10] *Gamber-Johnson, LLC v. Trans Data Net Corp.*, 2001 WI App 224.

[11] 17a-4(f)(2)(ii)(A).

[12] Section III(B) of SEC Release No. 34-44238, "Commission Guidance to Broker-Dealers on the Use of Electronic Storage Media under the Electronic Signatures in Global and National Commerce Act of 2000 with Respect to Rule 17a-4."

[13] SEC Release No. 34-47806, "Electronic Storage of Broker-Dealer Records," May 7, 2003.

4

Information Management Compliance (IMC)

In the first three chapters, we provided a framework for understanding Information Management and for identifying and managing business records. In this chapter we begin to explore the core concept of the book, Information Management Compliance (IMC).

What Is Compliance?

Although the term compliance is most often associated with the legal world, understanding it solely as a legal term is too narrow. In a broader context, and in the context used in this book, compliance simply means to act in accordance with any accepted standard or criteria. The "accepted standard" can refer to any kind of criteria, including business goals, performance measurements, laws, regulations, or quality targets.

In a general sense, there are two basic elements to compliance, namely:

1. Determining what the criteria should be
2. Developing techniques (often called *controls*) to ensure that the criteria are followed

Compliance is also a specific discipline that is practiced within dedicated departments in many regulated organizations around the world. These departments focus on ensuring that the organization complies with laws, regulations, codes, and other sources of compliance criteria. According to the International Compliance Association, organizational compliance departments have five key functions:[1]

1. To identify the risks that an organization faces and provide guidance on the identified risks.

2. To design and implement controls to protect an organization from those risks.
3. To monitor and report on the effectiveness of those controls.
4. To resolve compliance difficulties.
5. To advise the organization on risks, rules, and controls.

How Compliance and Information Management Fit Together

Although the compliance concept can apply to nearly any activity or department, in this book we are concerned with how to achieve compliance in Information Management.

IMC involves:

1. The development of Information Management criteria based on legal, regulatory, and business needs.
2. The implementation of controls designed to ensure compliance with those criteria.

To put it another way, IMC is a fusion of the Compliance discipline with Information Management activities. Although it may seem natural on one level to bring these two areas together, at most organizations Compliance and Information Management typically exist within different departments and exhibit very different cultures. Also, they often take fundamentally different approaches to the problem they are designed to address. That is, Information Management programs often take a *best practices* approach, while Compliance often is based on a *risk management* methodology.

Combining the Two Approaches

As each of those two approaches has strengths and limitations, organizations should employ the best of both in developing their IMC programs.

Information Management programs are typically developed with the objective of achieving a reasonable level of assurance that information will be effectively managed, with a minimum of overhead. Organizations try to achieve that objective by implementing a series of recommendations and practices that are generally accepted as highly effective yet not inordinately costly—commonly called *best practices*.

A weakness with this approach is that there really is no single set of best practices that is applicable to all organizations. Further, changes in the economy, operating environment, and technology can make current best practices obsolete.

On the other hand, Compliance tends to take a risk management–based approach. This approach involves identifying the risks that an organization faces; evaluating the potential for damage represented by each risk; and addressing these potentials in a systematic manner.

Common risk factors that an organization typically evaluate when building Compliance programs include:

- The nature and complexity of its business
- The diversity of its operations
- The scale, volume, and value of its business transactions
- The quantities or kinds of litigation
- Regulatory environment and oversight
- The nature and magnitude of risk-related activities

Risk management has its own pitfalls, as it depends on the ability of the organization not only to identify all possible risks but also to gauge the likelihood that a particular risk will occur and how often, and determine the appropriate amount of time and energy that should be spent protecting the organization against each risk. Making these judgments and calculations can be very difficult, particularly when addressing "soft" risks such as the chance that a company executive is going to indiscriminately destroy documents related to a trial. In addition, calculating the costs of efforts designed to prevent such eventualities, such as training programs and investments in "corporate culture," is also difficult. See the discussion of Total Cost of Failure (TCF) in Chapter 12.

This characterization of Information Management and Compliance is intentionally simplistic and does not capture the complex mix of strategies that most organizations employ in their Information Management and Compliance programs. The intent is to illustrate the need for organizations to use both best practice and risk management strategies in the development of their Information Management programs.

The process of IMC starts with a body of best practices and continues by adapting these practices to an organization's specific needs according to their unique legal, regulatory, business, and risk environment.

Sources of IMC Criteria

In Information Management, there are two broad categories of compliance criteria:

1. Criteria imposed on an organization from an *external* source such as a regulatory body. These include the following criteria:
   - **Laws**, such as Sarbanes-Oxley
   - **Regulations**, such as IRS and SEC Rules
   - **Industry standards** required by agreement or contract, such as ISO standards that must be followed when manufacturing products for export
2. Criteria voluntarily adopted or developed by an organization *internally*. These include such criteria as:
   - **Methods** developed internally or by industry associations, such as Total Quality Management™ or Six Sigma™, which companies adopt in order to improve internal operations
   - **Voluntary standards and codes** such as website accessibility standards for people with disabilities, published by the World Wide Web Consortium
   - **Operating procedures** developed and refined by an organization over its operating life because they are the most efficient, reflect the company's values, or simply because "that's the way we do things"

Establishing Your Compliance Criteria

Determining all of the criteria that your organization should (or must) comply with can be complex, especially if your organization is international (or subject to multiple jurisdictions) or is involved in many different lines of business. Table 4-1 shows some common examples of compliance criteria and the organizations that they affect.

Table 4-1: Organizations and Sources of Compliance Criteria

Type of Organization	Sources of Compliance Criteria
Commercial entities	Federal, state, and local laws and statutes governing business operations, such as tax laws and commercial codes
Government agencies	Government standards for performance, accountability, and reporting, such as those created by the U.S. Office of Management and Budget (OMB)
Public companies	Federal, state, and local laws governing the conduct of public companies, such as the Sarbanes-Oxley Act
Manufacturing companies	ISO 9000 series standards regarding manufacturing practices
Companies online	Web "privacy seals" such as TRUSTe, and privacy standards such as the Platform for Privacy Preferences, promulgated by the World Wide Web Consortium
Information technology companies	Technical standards, such as Department of Defense standards for electronic recordkeeping systems, and quality standards for suppliers to pharmaceutical companies

COMPLIANCE IS A PROCESS, NOT A PROJECT

Implementing new technology that has Information Management significance requires close attention to the ongoing compliance of the technology with criteria that support the goals of your Information Management program.

For example, many organizations embarking upon imaging projects (i.e., converting paper records to digital images) discover that there is far more to scanning and imaging than meets the eye. In fact, if done properly, the process may consist of numerous stand-alone activities—from proper document preparation, to the development of a comprehensible indexing regime, to a post-scan review to ensure complete capture and usability of the image. To get it right, organizations need to develop policies and procedures based on industry best practices or standards. These policies become the "compliance criteria" for making sure that employees know what to do to get it right every time, at every step of the process.

Continued

COMPLIANCE IS A PROCESS, NOT A PROJECT *(Continued)*

Thereafter, organizations must ensure that employees continue to get it right. Continued vigilance may require monitoring the actions of the employees, auditing to ensure that the captured images are of a high quality, and retraining employees regularly.

Unfortunately, companies have not been doing a good job in educating their employees on their IMC responsibilities. A 2008 Kahn Consulting survey indicated that, on average, only 15% of an organization's employees understand their responsibilities and how to fulfill them.[2]

If organizations think that the "imaging project" is over when the technology "goes live," they need to think again, because this attitude will likely mean an IMC breakdown is in their future.

In other words, compliance is a process, not a project.

Organizational Liability

YOU MAKE THE CALL

Which of the following information management compliance failures are true and which are false?

A. Federal agency is ordered to shut down its websites because of a lack of security controls that allows original government records to be altered, deleted, and so forth.

B. The Federal government will spend *billions* of dollars just looking for relevant information in a class action lawsuit.

C. Stolen army computers containing army secrets can be purchased at a market across from the base in an Arabic country.

D. Secret communications intercepted from known terror suspects, preceding the September 11 terror attacks, are purged before they are reviewed because of storage limitations.

E. All of the above.

If you answered E you are correct. All are true.

A corporation can only act through natural persons, and it is therefore held responsible for the acts of such persons fairly attributable to it. Charging a corporation for even minor misconduct may be appropriate where the wrongdoing was pervasive and was undertaken by a large number of employees or by all the employees in a particular role within the corporation...or was condoned by upper management.

On the other hand, in certain limited circumstances, it may not be appropriate to impose liability upon a corporation, particularly one with a compliance program in place, under a strict respondeat superior theory for the single isolated act of a rogue employee. There is, of course, a wide spectrum between these two extremes, and a prosecutor should exercise sound discretion in evaluating the pervasiveness of wrongdoing within a corporation.

Federal Prosecution of Business Organizations, U.S. Department of Justice[3]

Organizations, as well as individuals, can be tried and convicted for breaking the law. There are many reasons why an organization could be found liable. In many cases, a company is taken to task because it failed to employ adequate policies, supervision, training, discipline, corrective action, or other controls designed to diminish the likelihood of wrongdoing. In these cases the problem is seen to be so systemic that the organization must be punished in order to provide restitution to those damaged by its failure, and to ensure that its practices change.

A legal principle or doctrine called *respondeat superior* is commonly used by the courts to determine whether or not an organization should be held liable for the illegal acts performed by, or the damages caused by, its employees. Under this doctrine, an organization can be held "vicariously liable," providing that an employee's actions "(i) were within the scope of his duties and (ii) were intended, at least in part, to benefit the corporation."[4] Many cases where organizations were held liable for the Information Management failures and bad acts of its employees are explored throughout this book.

When federal prosecutors are faced with fraud and other criminal activity within corporations, they consider a number of factors when deciding whether to prosecute the corporation in addition to the individuals directly responsible for the wrongdoing.

These factors, which are provided in a manual for U.S. federal prosecutors (quoted above),[4] include:

1. The nature and seriousness of the offense.
2. The pervasiveness of wrongdoing within the corporation, including the complicity in, or condoning of, the wrongdoing by corporate management.
3. The corporation's history of similar conduct.
4. The corporation's timely and voluntary disclosure of wrongdoing and its willingness to cooperate in the investigation of its agents.
5. The existence and adequacy of the corporation's compliance program.
6. The corporation's remedial actions.
7. Collateral consequences, including disproportionate harm to shareholders and employees not proven personally culpable.
8. The adequacy of the prosecution of individuals responsible for the corporation's malfeasance.
9. The adequacy of remedies such as civil or regulatory enforcement actions.

A Case Study in IMC Failure: Morgan Stanley

The importance of establishing a culture of information management compliance is particularly important in heavily regulated industries, such as the securities industry. The example of Morgan Stanley provides a microcosm of how not to address (and how to address) compliance issues.

The Coleman Case

Probably the most well known of Morgan Stanley's compliance problems arose out of the suit by financier Ronald O. Perelman against the investment bank arising out of its advice to the appliance maker Sunbeam in Sunbeam's purchase of Perelman's camping goods business, the Coleman Company. The focus shifted from the plaintiff's allegations of fraud to Morgan Stanley's discovery violations.

The plaintiff sought information from Morgan Stanley's internal files, including electronic mail, from the outset of the litigation. Although Morgan

Stanley instructed its personnel to preserve paper files relating to the suit, it continued its normal practice of recycling, and thus overwriting, its e-mail tapes after 12 months, despite an SEC regulation requiring that all e-mails be retained in an easily accessible format for two years. The court found that several certifications that Morgan Stanley made in the course of producing e-mails were false. For example, when it produced 1,300 pages of e-mails pursuant to a court order in May 2004, and certifying that it had produced all relevant e-mails, there were over 2,100 backup tapes that had not been searched.

Morgan Stanley continued to find additional backup tapes after certifying that it had found all relevant material, up through February, 2005. It also subsequently reported flaws in the coding for the search protocols they had written, resulting in an additional 7,000 e-mails to be reviewed. The court summarized Morgan Stanley's deficiencies as follows:

> In sum, despite MS & Co's affirmative duty arising out of the litigation to produce its e-mails, and contrary to federal law requiring it to preserve the e-mails, MS & Co. failed to preserve many e-mails and failed to produce all e-mails required by the Agreed Order. The failings include overwriting e-mails after 12 months; failing to conduct proper searches for tapes that may contain e-mails; providing a certificate of compliance known to be false when made and only recently withdrawn; failing to timely notify CPH [plaintiff] when additional tapes were located; failing to use reasonable efforts to search the newly discovered tapes; failing to timely process and search data... or notify CPH of the deficiency; failing to write software scripts consistent with the Agreed Order; and discovering the deficiencies only after CPH was given the opportunity to check MS & Co's work and the MS & Co's attorneys were required to certify the completeness of the prior searches. Many of these failings were done knowingly, deliberately, and in bad faith.[6]

As a result of Morgan Stanley's actions, the court imposed a number of sanctions upon the company. First, the court elected to have a statement read to the jury detailing Morgan Stanley's discovery conduct. It also took the unusual step of reversing the burden of proof of some aspects of the case— Morgan Stanley was required to establish that it was *not* aware of fraudulent conduct and did not conspire with Sunbeam to defraud the plaintiff, instead of the plaintiff being required to establish that Morgan Stanley did. The plaintiff would be allowed to argue that Morgan Stanley's concealment of its role in the underlying transaction could be considered evidence of malice, or evil intent, which could form the basis for punitive damages.

Even after the entry of this order, the plaintiff discovered more discovery problems. For example, other software problems, hitherto unmentioned, had further reduced the number of e-mails processed by Morgan Stanley. Further evidence of misleading and false statements and certifications were established by the plaintiff. More than 6,800 additional backup tapes were found. The court therefore granted, in part, the plaintiff's later motion for default judgment.

The net effect of these orders resulted in a $1.58 billion jury verdict against Morgan Stanley. Although ultimately reversed by Florida appellate courts on other grounds, the case represents an example of how discovery issues can overshadow (and overwhelm) the underlying substantive issues in a case.

The IMC failures in the Coleman case magnified its impact. Because Morgan Stanley did not know where all of its backup tapes were, they were continually discovering new tapes. This continuing pattern of finding new tapes, along with their obfuscation, wore out the patience of the court and was a significant factor in the award of punitive damages (which accounted for over $800 million of the judgment).

The opinions do not even touch on the direct costs to Morgan Stanley in undertaking the search. Untold man-hours were spent searching for the tapes and loading the tapes into the archive. If there was no record retention policy (the court opinions do not mention one), then the company and its attorneys would be forced to wade through useless information with no business value, or information that may have had value at one time but should have been disposed of. Dealing with backup tapes themselves as an archival medium imposes additional costs. Tapes are designed for recovery of computers, not long-term information storage. Trying to find relevant information on a tape is an arduous, time-consuming process.

Other E-Mail Challenges

Similar allegations by the Securities and Exchange Commission resulted in the payment by Morgan Stanley in 2006 of a $15 million fine as a result of Morgan Stanley's failure to search for and produce e-mails in response to several SEC investigations between 2000 and 2005.[7] The SEC alleged that Morgan Stanley overwrote backup tapes and "made numerous misstatements regarding the status and completeness of its productions; the unavailability of certain documents; and its efforts to preserve requested e-mail."

Failure to Monitor for Possible Insider Trading

About the same time, the SEC settled a proceeding against Morgan Stanley for failure to monitor trading by its employees with possession of material nonpublic information regarding Morgan Stanley's clients. For example, as a result of miscoding and mislabeling, Morgan Stanley failed to monitor about 434,000 employee or employee-related accounts for trading in so-called "Watch List" securities. Thus, the SEC found that:

> *Despite the legal requirements to do so, Morgan Stanley, for years, failed to maintain and enforce adequate written policies and procedures to prevent the misuse of material nonpublic information by Morgan Stanley or persons associated with it. Due to a systemic breakdown in this critical compliance function, Morgan Stanley failed to conduct any surveillance of a massive number of accounts and securities. Moreover, Morgan Stanley's written policies failed to provide adequate guidance to Morgan Stanley personnel charged with conducting surveillance, and there were inadequate controls in place with respect to certain aspects of Watch List maintenance.[8]*

System Compliance Problems

In 2007, the SEC settled a proceeding with Morgan Stanley in which Morgan Stanley agreed to disgorge profits in the total amount of about $6.4 million, and pay a $1.5 million penalty, in connection with discrepancies found by the SEC in some of its trading systems.[9] In some cases, the system embedded markups and markdowns in certain retail orders. In other cases, the operation of the system resulted in delays, in violation of their duty to execute certain orders immediately.

An interesting aspect of the Commission's order was its description of the interaction between system programmers and compliance personnel. Although compliance officials had discovered some initial programming problems (which were corrected), Morgan Stanley "had no procedure requiring

Compliance's approval of changes to the market-making system by Information Technology personnel. As a result, Compliance's knowledge and understanding of specific programming changes, and their intended and actual effects, was either incomplete or non-existent." Although the programmers provided comments in plain English in their code, no one in either the Compliance, IT, or the business units reviewed the comments, which the SEC found might have prevented some of the failures.

To Morgan Stanley's credit, the SEC described several incidents where discovered problems were promptly acted upon. In December, 2004, an employee discovered some discrepancies in prices that should have been identical. Although the differences were sub-pennies, the employee brought the issue to the attention of an attorney, "who advised that the cause needed to be understood and resolved promptly." The employee made efforts to do so. About a week later, a trader noticed an unusual amount of profit ($400,000) made in a few minutes of unusually volatile trading. He immediately brought the matter to the attention of his manager and system support personnel. By that afternoon, the problem was pinpointed, and the system code was changed to eliminate any markups or markdowns on the affected retail orders. Morgan Stanley also "immediately cancelled and rebilled the affected trades." In addition, Morgan Stanley "performed an internal investigation into the matter and enhanced its supervision and controls over the relevant trading technology." These remedial efforts were considered by the SEC in its settlement of the dispute.

In the settlement itself, Morgan Stanley agreed to the appointment of an independent compliance consultant to "conduct a comprehensive review of [Morgan Stanley's] automated retail order handling practices to ensure that [Morgan Stanley] is complying with its duty of best execution to retail customers' orders." The consultant would make recommendations for changes and improvements to Morgan Stanley's policies and make a report to the SEC. If Morgan Stanley disagreed with any of the changes, it would have to propose an alternative to achieve the same purpose. An independent distribution consultant would also be appointed to develop a plan to distribute the $6.4 million disgorgement.

Conclusions

The above examples may unfairly portray Morgan Stanley as a poster child for information management compliance failures. In fact, as a multi-billion-dollar enterprise heavily dependent upon information systems for its day-to-day operations, the company should probably be commended for having as few failures as it has. In particular, the actions taken upon learning of its system problems in December, 2004 indicate that a culture of compliance has taken strong root at Morgan Stanley.

The advent of the personal computer and its widespread use in business have brought information management issues to even the mom-and-pop business. The danger is that complacency can develop from an overreliance and unquestioning acceptance of the results of computer systems.

The lesson learned is that compliance failures can impose very real costs upon a company, and not only in direct monetary outlays; they can affect a company's reputation and may subject the enterprise to higher levels of regulatory scrutiny. The objective of this book is to help companies develop a culture of compliance where compliance issues do not occur, but if they do, they can be caught and fixed before they become compliance problems.

Notes

[1] International Compliance Association, "Compliance and the Regulatory Environment." Online at http://www.int-comp.org/doc.asp?docId=6920&CAT_ID=676

[2] "GRC, E-Discovery, and RIM: State of the Industry—A Kahn Consulting, Inc. Survey in association with ARMA International, BNA Digital Discovery and E-Evidence, Business Trends Quarterly, and the Society of Corporate Compliance & Ethics." Online at www.kahnconsultinginc.com/library/surveys.html

[3] "Federal Prosecution of Business Organizations," Department of Justice Memorandum to Heads of Department Components and United States Attorneys, January 2003.

[4] Ibid.

[5] Ibid.

[6] *Coleman (Parent) Holdings, Inc. v. Morgan Stanley & Co., Inc.*, No. 502003CA005045XXOCAI (Fla. Cir. Ct., March 1, 2005)

[7] U.S. Securities and Exchange Commission, "Morgan Stanley Sued for Repeated E-Mail Production Failures; Morgan Stanley Agrees to Pay a $15

Million Penalty and Undertake Reforms in Settlement," Litigation Release No. 19693, May 10, 2006.

[8] Order, In the Matter of Morgan Stanley & Co., Inc. and Morgan Stanley DW Inc., Admin. Proceeding File No. 3-12342 (Securities and Exchange Comm., June 27, 2006).

[9] Order, In the Matter of Morgan Stanley & Co., Inc., Admin. Proceeding File No. 3-12631 (Securities and Exchange Comm., May 9, 2007).

5

Achieving IMC: Introduction to the Seven Keys

In Chapter 4 we introduced the concept of IMC, and discussed how the concepts of Compliance and Information Management fit together to provide a new approach to Information Management. Here we will introduce the Seven IMC Keys, which form the basis of a methodology for all organizations to follow.

The Facts: Something Is Broken

FACT: In 2006, a federal district court threw out a dealership's case against a car manufacturer where the dealership willfully withheld its computer system containing financial data from the manufacturer, and one of the principals deliberately lied about its whereabouts when he knew the system had been repossessed. In affirming the dismissal in 2008, the Eighth Circuit Court of Appeals stated that "[p]laintiffs have behaved like a pack of weasels and can't expect any part of their tale to be believed."[1]

FACT: A bankruptcy court judge in 2007 found a bankruptcy trustee guilty of bad faith destruction of evidence when he installed "GhostSurf" software on a computer prior to turning it over to the government. The judge also threatened the trustee with jail time if he did not turn over other computer equipment and data to the government.[2]

FACT: The Nuclear Regulatory Commission ordered changes in a nuclear plant located in San Onofre, California after discovering that a fire watch worker had falsified records and skipped hourly rounds on many occasions over five years.[3]

FACT: In 2008, the State of Texas initiated proceedings to recover $26 million in overpayment from charter schools as a result of falsified or inaccurate attendance records.[4]

FACT: A director of a UK trucking firm was sentenced to 15 months in prison in 2008 for 250 counts of falsifying records from speed and distance measuring devices on the firm's trucks.[5]

Allegations of records destruction, mismanagement, and falsification abound, implicating numerous companies. Billions of dollars have been erased from stock valuations, careers and reputations have been shattered, and companies have disappeared completely.

What Exactly Is Broken?

What is wrong with the way that these and other organizations are managing their information assets? Although it is difficult to narrow it down to a single set of causes in every case, there are some common elements in the failures that we have seen in the first part of this new millennium, and that continue to this day.

1. The natural result of market contraction/correction

In the boom years of the 1990s, compliance was not a high priority in all organizations. Times were good, everyone was making money, and competitive pressures to build market share and compete for a place in "the new economy" were extremely high. Many regulators couldn't keep up with the number of new companies, the new kinds of businesses activities, and the rapid pace of technology adoption.

However, as the market changes, so does the business climate. Today there is a greater focus on corporate accountability, compliance, transparency, ethics, and good governance. New accounting standards have been written and new laws have been passed. Mistakes of the boom years are now catching up with many companies as IMC activities they neglected and shortcomings they overlooked in the past are coming to light.

2. The rush to technology

Although this point is closely related to the last one, there is a separate issue that is also important. Over the past decade, enterprise software and hardware spending has grown at historically unseen rates. Many new technologies have been developed, many of them centered around the ubiquity and low cost of network connectivity offered by the Internet. As the market heated up, organizations felt even greater pressure to adopt new technologies to ensure that competitors were not gaining an advantage in their ability to meet customer expectations. In the rush to technology, "boring old" Information Management issues such as records retention often fell by the wayside. Today, the failure to confront those issues at the outset is causing problems for many organizations.

3. The design of information technology itself

In the same way that organizations in the past decade were not overly concerned about the IMC implications of new technology before implementing it, most enterprise technology was not designed with IMC in mind. Voicemail systems make it difficult to retain voicemail messages, even though they may have contractual or other legal significance. E-mail systems allow routine purging even though they likely contain valuable and legally significant information. Web forms and electronic documents separate content from presentation, making it difficult to capture and store a complete and accurate record. E-mail messages can be intercepted and altered with ease. Digital storage media have relatively short life spans and are subject to corruption. The list goes on and on.

Many vendors are responding to these needs by building in features that make it easier to capture and retain records. A recent example can be found in the ongoing maturation of instant messaging, which has evolved from a tool for kids, with no inherent security or retention capabilities, to an enterprise tool with a variety of configuration options for achieving IMC.

4. Authority and responsibility

Over the last two decades, as more and more company records and information were created and stored in electronic form, it became increasingly unclear exactly whose job it was to take responsibility for electronic records. What person in the organization understood archival science, Records Management, and how to configure the e-mail system for retention? Moreover, who had the authority to design, implement, fund, and operate a program that addressed both the old world and the new world issues? The result was (and continues to be) that many IMC issues have simply fallen through the cracks.

5. Lack of a holistic view

In many organizations, governance structures and cultures have failed to evolve to account for their overwhelming reliance on electronic information.

For example, the chief information officer typically sees his or her role strictly as building and maintaining the systems that house the information, and not taking responsibility for the information within those systems. The Records Management department typically is underfunded and understaffed. Meanwhile, backup tapes that contain e-mail records subject to subpoena are being overwritten, with or without criminal intent.

The result is the lack of a holistic view. Such a view starts with the understanding that an organization has Information Management obligations, then seeks to understand what Information Management criteria the organization must comply with, and finally implements controls to make sure such compliance happens. The GRC approach would not significantly differ in this context, as the additional risk management analysis demonstrates the risk of not achieving IMC.

The Federal Sentencing Guidelines

As we noted in the Introduction, we used a section of the *Federal Sentencing Guidelines* as a model in developing the Seven Keys to IMC, which form the heart of this book. This section (Chapter 8) of the *Guidelines* provides seven criteria that the courts will look at when sentencing a company that is found guilty of a criminal act. Further, the Department of Justice evaluates an organization's compliance with these seven criteria "when deciding whether to prosecute corporations."[6]

Since 1991, the *Federal Sentencing Guidelines* have:

> *Provided incentives for organizations to report violations, cooperate in criminal investigations, discipline responsible employees, and take the steps needed to prevent and detect criminal conduct by their agents. The guidelines mandate high fines for organizations that have no meaningful programs to prevent and detect criminal violations or in which management was involved in the crime. The guidelines take into account the potential range of organizational criminal culpability.*
>
> U.S. Sentencing Commission, the organization responsible for the Guidelines[7]

Since they were published, the *Guidelines* have been very influential on the way that companies design and implement compliance and corporate ethics programs. They have also been adopted in various ways by a number of federal regulatory agencies, including the Department of Health and Human

Services, the Environmental Protection Agency, and the Securities and Exchange Commission.[8]

The following perspectives emphasize the influence that the *Guidelines* have had:

> *The impact of the [the* Federal Sentencing Guidelines*] has reached well beyond the courtroom to broadly affecting corporate and organizational behavior. The Guidelines offer powerful incentives for corporations today to have in place compliance programs to detect violations of law promptly and to report violations to appropriate public officials when discovered, and to take voluntary remedial efforts. Any rational person attempting in good faith to meet an organizational governance responsibility would be bound to take into account...the enhanced penalties and the opportunities for reduced sanction that [the* Federal Sentencing Guidelines*] offer.*
>
> In re Caremark International Inc. Derivative Litigation[9]

> *The organizational guidelines have had a startling impact on the implementation of compliance and business ethics programs over the last ten years. These guidelines provide incentives for voluntary reporting and cooperation but punish an organization's failure to self-police. There is more interest than ever in these guidelines.*
>
> U.S. Sentencing Commission chair, Judge Diana E. Murphy[10]

It is easy to see why they have been so influential. Not only do the *Guidelines* tell companies how fines and penalties will be assessed, but they also help companies determine what they can do to help avoid or reduce sanctions for wrongdoing.

Although the original focus of the *Guidelines*' seven criteria, or keys, is on criminal misconduct, the keys are easily adapted to the world of IMC. In fact, not only are the seven keys adaptable, they are ideal for Information Management, and form the core of our IMC approach and methodology.

The intention in applying these Seven Keys to Information Management is not to provide an exact match between the way the keys are used in the criminal justice system and Information Management but rather to adopt the keys for Information Management.

Challenges to the Guidelines
Don't Diminish IM Relevance

In *U.S. v. Booker*,[11] the U.S. Supreme Court held that the use by federal judges of the *Federal Sentencing Guidelines* was no longer mandatory. Does this mean that the compliance structure set forth in Chapter 8 of the *Guidelines* was relegated to the trash heap? Absolutely not.

In *Booker,* the Supreme Court found a significant problem with the *Guidelines*. They permitted judges to increase sentences based on facts that were never presented to the jury. This directly conflicts with the Sixth Amendment's right to a trial by jury. The Court had previously held that "[i]f a State makes an increase in a defendant's authorized punishment contingent on the finding of a fact, that fact—no matter how the State labels it—must be found by a jury beyond a reasonable doubt."[12] How would the Court resolve the problem? Would it invalidate the *Guidelines* as a whole? Or would it invalidate only a portion of the *Guidelines*, letting the rest remain intact?

The Court took the former approach, by deleting the provision making the *Guidelines* mandatory. By invalidating two specific statutory sections, "the federal sentencing statute…makes the *Guidelines* effectively advisory."[13] The continuing validity of the *Guidelines* was emphasized in the Court's statement that sentencing courts are still required to consider *Guidelines* sentencing ranges.[14] The Court reinforced this view in *United States v. Rita,* 127 S. Ct. 2456 (2007), where it held that an appellate court can presume a sentence imposed within *Guidelines* ranges to be reasonable without violating the Sixth Amendment. Thus, as the courts are still required to consider *Guidelines* requirements in sentencing, Chapter 8 of the *Guidelines*, relating to sentencing of organizations, remains viable.

The Seven Keys

The Seven Keys of IMC are detailed below. Part II of this book is devoted to a detailed exploration of each of these Keys.

1. **Good Policies and Procedures.** Organizations must develop and implement policies and procedures designed to ensure that its Information Management Compliance responsibilities are addressed and its obligations are met.

2. **Executive-Level Program Responsibility.** Senior executives and managers must take overall responsibility for the Information Management program.

3. **Proper Delegation of Program Roles and Components.** Responsibility for the Information Management programs must be delegated only to those individuals with appropriate training, qualifications, and authority.

4. **Program Communication and Training.** The organization must take steps to effectively communicate Information Management policies and procedures to all employees. These steps might include, for example, requiring all employees to participate in training programs, and the dissemination of information that explains in a practical and understandable manner what is expected of employees.

5. **Auditing and Monitoring to Measure Program Compliance.** The organization must take reasonable steps to measure compliance with Information Management policies and procedures by utilizing monitoring and auditing programs.

6. **Effective and Consistent Program Enforcement.** Information Management program policies and procedures must be consistently enforced through appropriate disciplinary mechanisms and the proper configuration and management of Information Management–related systems.

7. **Continuous Program Improvement.** When improper management of information is detected, the organization must take all reasonable steps to respond appropriately to the activity and to prevent further similar activities—including any necessary modifications to its Information Management Program.

Notes

[1] *Ridge Chrysler Jeep, LLC v. DaimlerChrysler Services North America, LLC,*2006 U.S. Dist. LEXIS 63664 (N.D. Ill. Sept. 6. 2006), aff'd 516 F.3d 623 (8th cir. 2008).

[2] *U.S. v. Krause,* 367 B.R. 740 (Bankr. D. Kan. 2007).

[3] Craig Tenbroeck, "Fire watch specialist skipped rounds, falsified records at nuclear plant," *North County Times* (CA), Jan. 15, 2008,

http://www.nctimes.com/articles/2008/01/15/news/top_stories/
1_01_031_14_08.txt.

[4] Charter schools owe state $26 million for overstated attendance." *Waco Tribune-Herald* (wacotrib.com), April 7, 2008 http://www.wacotrib.com/news/content/news/stories/2008/04/07/04072008wacwacocharter.html

[5] David Harris, "Haulier gets 15 months for tacho offences," March 31, 2008, roadtransport.com http://www.roadtransport.com/Articles/2008/03/31/130216/haulier-gets-15-months-for-tacho-offences.html

[6] "Federal Prosecution of Corporations," Department of Justice Memorandum to Component Heads and United States Attorneys, June 16, 1999.

[7] United States Sentencing Commission News Release, "Sentencing Commission Convenes Organizational Guidelines Ad Hoc Advisory Group," Thursday, February 21, 2002.

[8] "Federal Prosecution of Corporations," Department of Justice Memorandum to Component Heads and United States Attorneys, June 16, 1999.

[9] In re Caremark International Inc. Derivative Litigation, Del. Chancery C.A. 13670, 698 A.2d 959, 970 (September 25, 1996).

[10] United States Sentencing Commission News Release, "Sentencing Commission Convenes Organizational Guidelines Ad Hoc Advisory Group," Thursday, February 21, 2002.

[11] 543 U.S. 220 (2005).

[12] *Id.* at 231, *citing Ring* v. *Arizona,* 536 U.S. 584, 602 (2002).

[13] 543 U.S. at 245.

[14] *Id.*

6 Sarbanes-Oxley and IMC

> *While Sarbanes-Oxley is financial legislation, at its heart it is about ensuring that internal controls or rules are in place to govern the creation and documentation of information in financial statements. Since its systems are used to generate, change, house and transport that data, CIOs have to build the controls that ensure the information stands up to audit scrutiny.*
>
> CIO magazine[1]

The Sarbanes-Oxley Act (SOX),[2] passed in the wake of the high-profile corporate scandals that filled the headlines in the opening years of this decade, is a complex piece of legislation with an enormous impact on IMC.

Organizations are spending a great deal of money and making major changes to ensure SOX compliance. As time passes, the changes are bearing fruit. In 2007, the average cost of complying with SOX section 404 was $1.7 million, according to Financial Executives International. These costs, however, represent a decline from the previous year.[3] Another survey reported internal control weaknesses down nearly 45% in the three years since SOX went into effect.[4]

While much of the discussion around SOX has focused on its impact on corporate governance, financial reporting, and accounting practices, the law's impact extends beyond these areas. In fact, the law goes to the heart of IMC by affecting the way that organizations must manage and control information.

As a law, SOX is designed to improve the accountability and transparency of public companies. Accountability and transparency depend upon trustworthy business records because trustworthy business records are the bedrock of accounting and financial reporting systems. For example, earnings figures are derived from documentation of business transactions—purchase orders, invoices, payment information, contracts, and so on. Obviously, if any of these records are inaccurate, the information in the accounting system will be, too. As a result, compliance with SOX relies on a foundation of Information Management practices designed to ensure the accuracy and trustworthiness of business records. In other words, Information Management Compliance.

This chapter discusses the impact of SOX on IMC. It is important to note that SOX is a complex law that creates many new legal obligations. Many of these obligations have no direct bearing on Information Management and address issues specific to the public accounting profession. Furthermore, as a practical matter, SOX required the SEC to amend and add to several of its existing rules and regulations, so much of the law's impact is felt through the SEC's regulations.[5] The focus of this Chapter is limited to those sections of SOX and related regulations that affect Information Management.

Doing Business in the Post-Sarbanes-Oxley Era: Everyone Is Affected

And today I sign the most far-reaching reforms of American business practices since the time of Franklin Delano Roosevelt. This new law sends very clear messages that all concerned must heed. This law says to every dishonest corporate leader: you will be exposed and punished; the era of low standards and false profits is over; no board-room in America is above or beyond the law.

U.S. President George W. Bush, signing the Sarbanes-Oxley Act, July 30, 2002[6]

Even though SOX is aimed at public companies and their auditors, all organizations should reassess their approach to Information Management in the context of SOX.[7] SOX came into being largely because elected officials saw existing laws as insufficient to protect the interests of the investing public, and because of a public outcry for the government to take action to prevent and punish corporate malfeasance. SOX was just one part of the U.S. federal government's efforts to address these issues. The President's Corporate Fraud Task Force, for example, was created in the same timeframe as SOX to "aggressively investigate and prosecute fraud," and has aided in obtaining "over 250 corporate fraud convictions or guilty pleas."[8]

Many of the high-profile cases of corporate malfeasance that ushered in the post-SOX era (including those discussed throughout this book) involved allegations of improper alteration and destruction of business information. As a result, issues of Information Management and corporate fraud have become linked in the minds of corporate boards, shareholders, and the public at large. All companies are affected by the heightened scrutiny of internal practices that characterizes the post-SOX business era.

Furthermore, Section 802 of SOX updates the criminal code to provide stiffer criminal penalties for those who destroy information "with the intent to impede, obstruct, or influence the investigation or proper administration of **any matter** within the jurisdiction of any department or agency of the United States." (emphasis added)[9] The scope of this language suggests that SOX Section 802 criminal penalties may apply to activities and situations that impact individuals in organizations beyond just public companies. Section 802 is explored below.

The overall affect of SOX and related events is a greater awareness of Information Management issues than ever before. There is a greater realization that a consistent and effective approach to Information Management is critical to gaining and maintaining the trust of partners, customers, regulators, and even employees. Consequently, all organizations—not just public companies—need to ensure that they are responding to the new realities of this era. Many private organizations have already adopted many of the principles of SOX and used them to reevaluate their approach to Information and Records Management. All organizations in the post-SOX era need to acknowledge the clear link between successful Information Management programs and business success as a whole.

Destruction and Alteration of Information: SOX Section 802

> *Whoever knowingly alters, destroys, mutilates, conceals, covers up, falsifies, or makes a false entry in any record, document, or tangible object with the intent to impede, obstruct, or influence the investigation or proper administration of any matter within the jurisdiction of any department or agency of the United States or any case filed under title 11, or in relation to or contemplation of any such matter*

or case, shall be fined under this title, imprisoned not more than 20 years, or both.

Sarbanes-Oxley Section 802 (emphasis added)

Section 802 is one of the more disconcerting sections of SOX and is likely the section that initially got the attention of most organizations when SOX was signed into law. Section 802 outlines dramatic criminal penalties for the improper destruction or alteration of business records. By doing so, SOX emphasizes the reality that reliable and accurate financial reporting depends on protecting the records, documents, and other evidence that provides the foundation for that financial information.

The *disposal* of business records is as integral a part of Information Management as *retention*. Disposal of records according to documented policies enables organizations to get rid of information that is costly to store and manage, without fear of raising the ire of the courts or regulators. However, organizations also have an obligation to suspend normal disposition practices in the face of anticipated or ongoing audits, investigations, litigation, and other proceedings—including matters contemplated by Section 802.

Consequently, organizations need a mechanism (commonly referred to as a Legal Hold mechanism) to inform employees of the need to preserve information. Such a mechanism should be built with the following principles in mind:

- **Decide who needs to be notified, and what they need to be told.** It is critical that the right people receive notification of the need to preserve information, and that they are provided with specific instructions on the kinds of information that must be preserved, and how it must be preserved. Notification may need to extend to contractors, outsourced storage providers, and other parties if they have responsive information (i.e., information related to the matter) in their possession, care, custody, or control.

- **All forms of information and tangible objects are included.** All recorded information regardless of the media it is stored on, and all tangible objects (such as lab samples) related to the matter must be preserved.

- **Immediate action.** The obligation to suspend normal disposition practices may start the instant an organization reasonably believes that it may become involved in matters covered by Section 802. Organizations should not wait for a subpoena or other formal request for information before taking action.

- **Many kinds of "matters."** Organizations should not assume that the preservation obligation is limited to court proceedings. Section 802 provides a very broad definition of circumstances that may require special preservation activities: "**any matter** within the jurisdiction of **any department or agency** of the United States or any case filed under title 11, or **in relation to or contemplation** of any such matter or case. [Emphasis added]"

- **Create and manage documentation.** Formal written policies and procedures outlining the preservation process and identifying the specific tasks and roles within the process should be created, retained, and managed as a business record. In addition, e-mail memos, forms, and other information used to disseminate preservation notices should be retained and managed as a business record.

- **It's not just about "destruction."** Section 802 prohibits a broad range of activities beyond mere destruction, including alteration, mutilation, concealment, covering up, and falsifying. Organizations need to ensure that their Legal Hold mechanism addresses such activities. For example, purposefully disposing of proprietary software that is needed to access records during an investigation might be considered "concealment." Furthermore, allowing employees to encrypt records and "lose" the decryption key could be considered "covering up." Simply stated, the law is broader than just destruction or shredding.

Internal Controls: The Role of Information Management in Financial Reporting and Corporate Governance

The concept of *internal controls* is central to SOX, and it has a direct bearing on IMC. Section 404 of SOX requires senior management to include an "internal control report" in each annual report that assesses the effectiveness of their "internal controls and procedures... for financial reporting."[10] In addition, Section 404 requires a company's auditor to "attest to and report on" this report—in other words, "to assess the assessment." Section 302 requires CEOs and CFOs to certify in their annual and quarterly reports that they are responsible for these internal controls.[11] Section 906 provides criminal penalties including jail terms and fines of up to 20 years and $5 million, respectively, for executives who certify false financial reports.[12]

In May, 2007, the SEC issued new guidance regarding the interpretation of Section 404. The Commission recommended that companies take a GRC approach to their financial controls by evaluating whether existing controls adequately address the risk that material misstatements in financial statements would be detected in a timely fashion, and that management should take a risk-based approach to the evaluation of evidence on the operation of their financial controls. This approach enables management to focus more compliance efforts on high-risk areas, while less stringent efforts can be used for lower-risk areas.[13]

Although the concept of internal controls as used in SOX is well known in the public accounting world, it is less well known in the Information Management world. However, in the post-SOX era, individuals with responsibility for Information Management in all organizations need to become familiar with this key SOX concept.

INTERNAL CONTROLS

The term *internal control* over financial reporting is defined as a process designed by, or under the supervision of [the company's senior executives] and effected by the [company's] board of directors, management and other personnel, to provide reasonable assurance **regarding the reliability of financial reporting** and the preparation of financial statements for external purposes in accordance with generally accepted accounting principles and includes those policies and procedures that:

1. **Pertain to the maintenance of records that in reasonable detail accurately and fairly reflect the transactions** and dispositions of the assets of the issuer;

2. **Provide reasonable assurance that transactions are recorded as necessary to permit preparation of financial statements** in accordance with generally accepted accounting principles, and that receipts and expenditures of the issuer are being made only in accordance with authorizations of management and directors of the issuer; and

3. Provide reasonable assurance regarding prevention or timely detection of unauthorized acquisition, use or disposition of the issuer's assets that could have a material effect on the financial statements.

Exchange Act 13a-15(f) (emphasis added in bold throughout)

This definition, which comes from a key SEC regulation implementing SOX,[14] makes clear that internal controls have a scope that extends to Information Management practices. As stated by the definition, internal controls include "policies and procedures" designed to ensure that critical records are managed in such as way that they "accurately and fairly reflect" an organization's business transactions. Further, these policies and procedures should "provide reasonable assurance that transactions are recorded as necessary" to support accurate financial reporting and good corporate governance. These goals and concepts should sound familiar to anyone with experience in designing and implementing Information and Records Management programs.

Although the concept of internal controls clearly encompasses the specialized tools and techniques employed in public accounting and financial reporting, it seems clear that Information Management policies, techniques, and programs are also a key form of internal control that organizations need to employ in order to have confidence in the statements made in their Section 404 "internal control report," statements and Section 302 certifications. Information Management programs are, after all, explicitly designed to ensure the trustworthiness and accuracy of records that document business activities and transactions.

Information Management and SOX

In the post-SOX era, organizations must ensure that their approach to Information Management is one that supports the organization's need for trustworthy and accurate financial information. Information Management programs must give executives comfort that the information they are certifying to comply with SOX is trustworthy, is accurate, and can be supported by the organization's own business records.

Information Management programs provide critical internal controls that are central to ensuring that an organization can meet SOX requirements for the reliability and accuracy of financial reporting. The integrity and accessibility of records and other business information must be protected at all times—a requirement that takes on even greater importance when an organization anticipates or is involved in audits, investigations, litigation, or other formal proceedings. Organizations need to have a mechanism for ensuring that the right people throughout the organization are informed of the need to preserve responsive information. A GRC analysis reaches the same conclusion.

Violations of SOX mandates result in regulatory sanctions and often adverse publicity, as well as negative consequences for the C-level officials certifying the various SOX-related documents. Thus, a high risk coefficient is assigned to development maintenance of the internal controls necessary to achieve SOX compliance.

INFORMATION MANAGEMENT PREPAREDNESS CHECKLIST

Here are some activities (not all by any means) that you might undertake to achieve IMC in your organization:

1. Educate employees regarding the ownership of company information—for example, who *owns* the information that a salesperson's enters on his or her laptop and handheld computers?
2. Provide employees with rules for the secure transmission of electronic information.
3. Develop a privacy policy for the organization's website, another privacy policy for employees' personal information that resides in human resources records, and a third privacy policy, if applicable, for personal information about individual customers, clients, or patients.
4. Use Document Management and Records Management software and require all employees who use that software to be trained regarding its proper use.
5. Provide employees (especially IT staff) with written procedures for properly scanning, imaging, indexing, and storing records from paper to optical disc.
6. Create, disseminate, monitor, and enforce compliance with an Information Management policy.
7. Give certain employees in each business unit responsibility for Records Management as part of their job description.

Records management is an activity historically viewed as the maintenance of the corporate library. Corporate records were identified, non-records were disposed of, the records were classified, utilized, moved off into storage, and then finally disposed of. As computers were introduced into the enterprise, records managers had to develop new strategies for dealing with electronic information, particularly in the area of trustworthiness. To an extent, those strategies are still being developed today, although a strong foundation has been laid for the management of electronic records. Electronically stored information has drastically changed the science of records management, to the point that a new term has been coined, *records and information management* (RIM).

Information management compliance takes RIM to a whole new level. The electronic age has raised expectations of lawmakers and regulators with regard to legal and regulatory mandates imposed upon organizations. While dealing with these new realities, the enterprise must also be able to assess new business risks, again created in part by the technology revolution. Compliance arose in an attempt to quantify these risks and develop strategies and techniques, in the form of business controls, for addressing, managing, and monitoring and reporting on them.

IMC combines compliance with information management disciplines to address these challenges. The marriage of the two areas is natural as corporate compliance is achieved in many areas through utilization of company records. The concept of Governance, Risk Management, and Compliance (GRC) brings some of these concepts to the executive suite, and seeks to influence corporate decisions. IMC makes explicit the fact that information assets are essential components of corporate compliance, and have a critical role in informing the company's risk assessments.

The following chapters are designed to assist those who want to establish an IMC culture in their organizations. Based upon the *Federal Sentencing Guidelines*, these seven keys establish a comprehensive framework for transforming a company into a firm which maximizes the value of its information assets, while enabling it to meet its legal and regulatory obligations.

Notes

[1] Worthen, Ben, "Your Risks and Responsibilities: You may think the Sarbanes-Oxley legislation has nothing to do with you. You'd be wrong," *CIO*, May 15, 2003.

[2] Pub. L. 107-204, 116 Stat. 745 (2002).

[3] FEI Survey: Average 2007 SOX Compliance Cost $1.7 Million, Financial Executives International, April 30, 2008.

[4] Matthew Kirdahy, "Sarbox Continues to Bite," Forbes.com, November 28, 2007; available at http://www.forbes.com/leadership/2007/11/28/sarbanes-oxley-survey-lead-govern-cx_mk_1128compliance.html

5 Including, for example, Regulation S-K, S-B, S-X, and Exchange Act Rules 13a-14, 13a-15, 15d-14 and 15d-15.

6 "President Bush Signs Corporate Corruption Bill," White House Office of the Press Secretary, July 30, 2002. Online at http://www.whitehouse.gov/news/releases/2002/07/20020730.html

7 The term "public company" is used broadly here to include a range of entities that come under the SEC's jurisdiction. There may be cases where private companies are affected, such as when they have a public bond offering, for example.

8 "President's Corporate Fraud Task Force Compiles Strong Record," White House Office of the Press Secretary Fact Sheet, July 22, 2003. Online at http://www.whitehouse.gov/news/releases/2003/07/20030722.html

9 Pub. L. 107-204, 116 Stat. 745 (2002), SEC. 802.

10 Ibid., SEC. 404.

11 Ibid., SEC. 302.

12 Ibid., SEC. 906.

13 Shepard Mullin Richter & Hampton, LLP, "Section 404 Updates: SEC Adopts New Interpretative Guidance and Rules, and PCAOB Adopts New Auditing Standard No. 5," May 25, 2007, available at http://www.corporatesecuritieslawblog.com/corporate-governance-section-404-updates-sec-adopts-new-interpretative-guidance-and-rules-and-pcaob-adopts-new-auditing-standard-no-5.html.

14 SEC Release No. 33-8328, "Management's Reports on Internal Control Over Financial Reporting and Certification of Disclosure in Exchange Act Periodic Reports," June 5, 2003.

Seven Keys to Information Management Compliance

Key #1

Good Policies and Procedures

Organizations must develop and implement policies and procedures designed to ensure that its Information Management Compliance responsibilities are addressed and its obligations are met.

Key Overview

Policies and procedures provide the foundation of every Information Management program. Policies are a manifestation of an organization's beliefs about Information Management, and they express an organization's commitment to sound management—an important message not only to employees but to the outside world as well.

7

The Purpose of Policies and Procedures

Laying the Foundation of IMC

> [T]he Court concludes that Bank One breached its duty to preserve documents by failing to establish a comprehensive document retention policy with the appropriate scope and by failing to properly disseminate the policy to its employees.

Larson v. Bank One Corp., 2005 U.S. Dist. LEXIS 42131 (N.D. Ill. Aug. 18, 2005)

In the case mentioned above, the company failed to create adequate policies for the preservation of evidence related to litigation, and as a result, the jury was specifically instructed about its wrongdoing. There have been countless other cases where organizations paid a price simply because they did not invest the time and money required to create a set of policies and procedures adequate to address their Information Management needs. Policies and procedures don't need to be complex—in fact, often the simpler they are, the better.

Policies and procedures are the management tools that an organization uses to codify and communicate its approach to Information Management. They serve a variety of legal, compliance, operational, and business purposes. And, in the context of IMC, they provide the *criteria* that the *program* itself must *comply with*.

The Difference between Policies and Procedures

Policies and procedures work together to provide a two-tiered set of directives and guidelines. While policies provide a high-level articulation of an organization's position on particular issues, procedures bring those positions down to earth by laying out specific actions and responsibilities.

Information Management policies, without procedures, may not provide sufficient detail and direction to work effectively as guidance to employees. For example, an Information Management policy may contain a statement like this:

> *Our company must retain evidence of our business transactions in order to comply with laws, regulations, and our business and operational requirements.*

A nice statement, but one that may be of little value or meaning to an employee trying to determine whether or not he or she should retain a particular e-mail message, voicemail message, or instant message.

Or what about the technologist trying to determine how to build an online application that allows customers to sign up for new services on the company's website? How should he or she build the application so that it captures and preserves information required by law, or to meet the company's operational requirements? Companies often face this issue when building web-based applications.

Questions like these can only be answered through clear and detailed procedures that implement the policy. Policies and practices may exist in separate documents, but not necessarily. For example, a Records Management manual often contains a combination of policy statements (such as the Records Management program's purpose) and specific directives (such as step-by-step instructions for retaining specific kinds of records).

Provide Clear Directives to Employees

Without clearly written and widely disseminated policies and procedures, how can an organization expect its employees to know what their Information

Management obligations are? It cannot, especially in larger organizations where consistency is an even larger challenge.

Good policies and procedures should:

- Provide insight to employees on what management believes is important, thereby helping to establish the organization's culture and to set employee and management expectations.
- Clarify in plain language what each employee's Information Management obligations are, why the obligations exist, and what will happen if the employee fails to follow the directives.
- Provide consistent guidelines for employee behavior that last beyond the residency of a particular manager or executive. In this sense, policies and procedures are part of the soul of an organization—they continue to live on long past their authors, and provide a compass for ongoing organizational behavior.

Making a Statement to the World

Written policies and procedures make a statement to the outside world that an organization cares strongly about an issue. Widely disseminating policies and training employees on their implementation serves to emphasize an organization's commitment to addressing Information Management issues.

Making this statement to the outside world is not just a public relations strategy. In fact, it can be an important mitigating factor when mistakes do happen. If an organization can demonstrate to an investigator, regulator, court, or even the media that they had a policy in place and trained employees to follow the policy, then isolated failures are much more likely to be seen as individual accidents rather than organizational failures.

In the Larson case quoted at the beginning of this chapter, the court was seemingly angry not because employees destroyed relevant evidence, but rather because the company failed to have policies and procedures in place that would have helped to prevent the destruction. The judge stated, in part:

> The destruction or loss of several categories of documents reflects "extraordinarily poor judgment" and the failure to create and disseminate an ample document retention policy evinces "gross negligence" of Bank One's duties to preserve documents in the face of the

> *Larson litigation....However, there is no evidence that Bank One*
> *willfully destroyed any documents....A party has the right to pros-*
> *ecute its case in the way it deems fit based on all available relevant*
> *evidence...destroying or blindly allowing lower employees to destroy*
> *evidence that is crucial to one side's chosen theory, but not to the*
> *other side's theory, is rife with material prejudice.[1]*

Would the judge have permitted a damaging jury instruction if the company's policies and procedures had demonstrated that it took reasonable steps to ensure that it would consistently meet its Information Management obligations? Not as likely.

Not Following Your Own Policy Is Bad Policy

There are many cases in which having the right policies and procedures but not following them is as bad or perhaps worse than not having policies or procedures in the first place. This is clearly demonstrated in *Kentucky Cent. Life Ins. Co. v. Jones*,[2] where a dispute over the accuracy of the defendant's medical records resulted from failing to follow hospital policy.

The hospital where the defendant was a patient had a policy that required the admitting doctor to dictate the patient's case history within 48 hours. However, the doctor in this case failed to follow the policy, only providing the information five weeks later. This delay created an opportunity for the argument that the medical records were not trustworthy and accurate, and as such should not be admitted in evidence.

The very existence of the dictation policy suggests that the hospital itself believed that adherence to the policy was necessary to prevent lapses in the doctor's memory from reducing the accuracy of patient records. If this was the hospital's logic, as borne out by the policy, then why should they not be held accountable to that logic in the context of a dispute?

Furthermore, while the intent of the policy seems sound, it also seems that there was not an adequate system in place to ensure that the policy was followed. Aside from the potential risk to patients, this failure resulted in longer and more expensive litigation, as the parties had to address the veracity of the records at issue.

If You Don't Do It, Someone Else Will ─────

SEC, NYSE, NASD Fine Five Firms Total of $8.25 Million for Failure to Preserve Email Communications

The Securities and Exchange Commission, the New York Stock Exchange and NASD today announced joint actions against five broker-dealers for violations of recordkeeping requirements regarding e-mail communications. The firms consented to the imposition of fines totaling $8.25 million, along with a requirement to review their procedures to ensure compliance with record-keeping statues and rules.[3]

Five large Wall Street firms were fined $8.25 million for failing to properly preserve and manage e-mail communications pertaining to their business. The SEC ordered each company to review their e-mail management procedures and to prove within 90 days "it has established systems and procedures reasonably designed to achieve compliance with the statute and rules relating to e-mail retention."

When the SEC fined these firms, it provided detailed information on its areas of concern. Examine your own Information Management policies, procedures, and practices against these all-too-common issues.

- **No procedures and controls**. "Each firm had inadequate procedures and systems to retain and make accessible e-mail communications."
- **No management guidance or system provision**. "While some firms relied on employees to preserve copies of the e-mail communications on the hard drives of their individual personal computers, there were no systems or procedures to ensure that employees did so."
- **Backup is not retention**. Some firms said that they were backing up e-mail for disaster recovery or business continuity purposes, but "these firms discarded or recycled and overwrote their back-up tapes and other media, often a year or less after back-up occurred." (Note that the SEC requires brokers' e-mail "communications" to be retained for a minimum of three years.)

- **Lack of uniform procedures**. When the firms did retain e-mail, the e-mail was "often stored in an unorganized fashion on back-up tapes, other media, or on the hard drives of computers used by individual employees."
- **Departing employees**. "In some instances, hard drives of computers preserving electronic mail communications were erased when individuals left the employment of the firm."

While the fines in this case were not inconsequential, the more damaging and costly result in the long run may be the fact that regulators are now poised to watch the firms' every move.

Putting It Down in Writing

Policies and procedures are formal, written documents that are carefully managed and disseminated to ensure that their contents stay up to date and accurate. There is a reason for this formality.

Policies and procedures serve to formally document and provide proof of an organization's commitment and practices at a particular time, should there be a dispute in the future about its intent. The need for this formality may be less in smaller organizations, where the daily contact between supervisors and employees may allow company directives to be disseminated more informally.

The courts have recognized this distinction between large and small companies. For example, in *Faragher v. City of Boca Raton*,[4] the court acknowledged that "the employer of a small workforce" might expect that its duty to exercise "sufficient care" to provide a safe workplace "could be exercised informally," whereas an employer with many departments and "far-flung" employees would require a "formal policy."

There are two primary ways that an organization "speaks" in the course of investigations and litigation: through its employees and through its business records. Policies and procedures not only provide standards for how employees should behave when acting on the organization's behalf, they tell a story about the organization's priorities, commitment, and actions, which is important in the legal context.

A CASE FOR FORMALITY

A pharmaceutical company's IT department creates a new workflow application that is designed to make the process of new drug applications much faster and more efficient by eliminating paper. Instead of using handwritten signatures, system users are given user ID and passwords that they can type into the system to affix an "electronic signature" on a digital document.

The employees are given a quick briefing on how to use the system, which includes a warning (not in writing) that their electronic signatures are for their use only and are not to be shared with other employees.

A few weeks later, working under a tight deadline, an employee named Theodore tries to access the system. After trying to enter his password three or four times, he realizes that he forgot his password, and shouts over the cubicle to Dylan to get his user ID and password. Theodore then uses Dylan's password to access and digitally sign an important application for FDA approval.

The next month, during an FDA investigation, a question arises about that particular application. The FDA wants to know who signed the document. The log files show that Dylan signed the document, but he claims that he knows nothing about it. He then remembers that Theodore "borrowed" his password one day. Questions about the identity of the signer call the entire electronic signature system into question, the FDA investigation intensifies, and sanctions are assessed. Dylan is fired for sharing his password in violation of company policy.

Dylan then sues the company for wrongful termination. In the ensuing litigation, the company can provide no convincing evidence that it ever had a policy forbidding the sharing of user IDs and passwords. Dylan wins his case, and the company pays—a double whammy that could have been easily prevented by putting into writing, and preserving, the oral admonition that the company gave to employees during training for the new system.

For more information about password policies and how they can be enforced, see Chapter 18.

Limiting Corporate Liability for Employee Actions

One of the primary goals of compliant Information Management policies and procedures is to help organizations avoid liability for their employees' actions.

The legal doctrine of vicarious liability holds a company responsible for the acts of their employees found to be in furtherance of the company's business. Notwithstanding this doctrine, exceptions exist that may permit organizations to limit the liability caused by the "bad acts" of their employers.

Scenario 1: Pornography Sent Through Instant Messaging

Consider a fictional (but all too real) scenario where a female employee receives a pornographic image from a male employee through the company's instant messaging (IM) system, and files a harassment complaint. The company has an "electronic communications policy" that stipulates "the company's IM system cannot be used to send, receive, or display pornographic or violent images." The company also provides procedures in the employee manual for filing a complaint about any violation of company policy. The human resources department responds to the complaint by firing the employee who sent the offensive image.

In the ensuing wrongful termination dispute, the existence of the policy and the complaint procedure is likely to mitigate the liability attached to the company for the act of "harassment" by the employee who contravened the policy. While the company may not completely escape sanctions for the harassment, the damages will likely be much less that they otherwise would be.

Scenario 2: The Unencrypted E-Mail

In this fictional scenario, a hospital creates a new policy to respond to the new requirements of the Health Insurance Portability and Accountability Act (HIPAA). Among other things, the new policy requires "that any e-mail containing personal identifiable information be encrypted when sent outside the company firewall."

An employee accidentally misaddresses an unencrypted e-mail message intended for Patient A, and it end up in Patient B's inbox, unencrypted. Patient A is outraged and files a complaint, claiming that the hospital has violated the privacy of medical information in its possession.

During the ensuing dispute, the hospital provides a copy of the policy requiring encryption. It cannot, however, provide any convincing evidence that it ever trained employees how to use the encryption features of its e-mail software, or even ensure that each employed had access to the appropriate encryption software.

In this case, although the existence of a policy may provide some mitigation of liability, the company's failure to follow through with policy implementation, procedures, and training will not work in its favor. It will be harder for the company to argue that the release of private records to the wrong person was simply a mistake on the part of a single employee.

You Make The Call:

In this litigation environment, to be on the safe side, when should employees stop following the routine records retention rules and start to preserve any potentially relevant information pursuant to a Legal Hold?

1. When the company gets served with a lawsuit.
2. When the company anticipates or feels a lawsuit is imminent or threatened.
3. The company need not worry about it if their records retention rules are good.

If you answered 2, that is the best answer. In *Washington Alder LLC v. Weyerhaeuser*,[5] the court concluded that a threatening letter to sue for antitrust was sufficient to put the company on notice to preserve information responsive to the matter.

The Legal Hold

One of the most important concepts in electronic discovery is the *Legal Hold*. Once a party is aware (or should be aware) of the existence of a lawsuit, that party has the obligation to preserve documents relevant to the lawsuit.[6] How does a company "become aware" of a lawsuit, and how can the firm make sure that the proper documents will be preserved? Good policies and procedures are essential to the successful implementation of a legal hold.

In many cases, legal counsel is the first to become aware of a lawsuit, when a demand letter from an attorney is received, stating the intent to file a lawsuit and requesting that documents (including electronic documents) be preserved. However, in other situations, courts have found that the duty to preserve documents arises before this happens. In *Zubulake v. UBS Warburg*[7] the court concluded the duty to preserve had arisen before Ms. Zubulake had filed a charge with the Equal Employment Opportunity Commission because of an e-mail sent by one of her coworkers to other coworkers and supervisors that "essentially called for Zubulake's termination." The only way that a company has even a chance of learning about these types of situations is through policies and procedures designed to facilitate the reporting of such incidents to management and/or legal counsel.

The process does not stop here. Once incidents are reported, and the determination is made that a lawsuit is possible and relevant documents must be preserved, employees need guidance on how to properly preserve documents. This is particularly important in terms of electronic documents. Although employees can easily press the delete key, such documents don't necessarily disappear—they just become more difficult to retrieve. Don't forget about an audit process. A successful legal hold shouldn't depend upon an employee remembering to read the second page of a spreadsheet. A good legal hold policy and implementing procedures will:

- Contain a process by which management and/or legal counsel can be notified regarding possible litigation
- Describe the legal hold notification process (the "legal hold notice")
- Describe the types of information subject to the hold
- Instruct employees on the proper preservation of documents
- Relate the consequences of the failure to preserve or the deliberate destruction of documents
- Provide for the periodic reissuance of the legal hold notice to remind affected employees of their continuing duty to preserve documents
- Provide for an auditing process to make sure the appropriate documents are in fact being preserved
- Allow for periodic review and termination of Legal Holds
- The consequences of a failure to establish a Legal Hold can vary. The case itself can be dismissed,[8] juries can be instructed about the party's failure to preserve documents,[9] certain facts of the opposing party's case can be deemed proven,[10] and costs can be shifted to the offending party.[11]

Notes

[1] *Larson v. Bank One Corp.*, 2005 U.S. Dist. LEXIS 42131 (N.D. Ill. Aug. 18, 2005).

[2] *Kentucky Cent. Life Ins. Co. v. Jones*, 1993 U.S. App. LEXIS 21976.

[3] "SEC, NYSE, NASD Fine Five Firms Total of $8.25 Million for Failure To Preserve E-Mail Communications," SEC press release, December 03, 2002.

[4] *Faragher v. City of Boca Raton*, 524, U.S. 775 (1998).

[5] *Washington Alder LLC v. Weyerhaeuser*, 2004 U.S. Dist. LEXIS 8756 (D. Ore. May 7, 2004).

[6] *Zubulake v. UBS Warburg*, 220 F.R.D. 212 (S.D.N.Y. 2003).

[7] Ibid.

[8] *Leon v. IDX Systems Corp.*, 464 F.3d 951 (9th Cir. 2006).

[9] *Wells v. Berger, Newmark & Fenchel, P.C.*, 2008 U.S. Dist. LEXIS 21608 (N.D. Ill. Mar. 18, 2008).

[10] *APC Filtration, Inc. v. Becker*, 2007 U.S. Dist. LEXIS 76221 (N.D. Ill. Oct. 12, 2007).

[11] *Padgett v. City of Monte Sereno*, 2007 U.S. Dist. LEXIS 24301 (N.D. Cal. Mar. 20, 2007).

8

Making Good Policies and Procedures

In the last chapter we looked at the need for Information Management policies and procedures. In this chapter we will look at strategies that organizations can use to make good policies and procedures that address their IMC needs.

Create a Policy and Procedure Structure

In smaller organizations, a single policy document may be enough to address most Information Management issues. However, most medium and large organizations will require a number of different policy and practice documents to adequately address the Information Management needs of different departments and different operations.

As such, organizations need to make sure that they not only have the right policies and procedures, but also that these various documents work together as seamlessly as possible. This can be challenging in complex environments where there are many departments with diverse needs.

Each organization will take a different approach to Information Management policies and procedures, based on a number of factors, including the nature of its business, its organizational culture, and its regulatory environment. In other words, there is no standard, one-size-fits-all policy.

Records Management Policies and Procedures

There are several ways to structure the policies and procedures of a Records Management program, but there are also many consistent elements. For example, they should start with broad, high-level policies that govern the entire organization. Here are some examples of high-level policy tools:

1. **High-Level Information Management and Records Management Policy Manual.** This policy provides high-level, principle-based guidance for the entire organization, and provides the minimum standards that must be followed by all departments and groups. It is the foundation of all other policies and procedures created or adopted throughout the organization. Thus, it needs to be broad enough to accommodate different needs, yet specific enough to provide useful guidance.

2. **Organizational Retention Rules.** A detailed document that provides retention periods for different categories of records in the organization, and indicates the legal, regulatory, or business reasons for each retention period.

3. **Electronic Records Policy.** Although it may be appropriate to address specific electronic records issues in the general Records Management policy, it may also be necessary to create a separate policy to address specific electronic records issues. A separate document can be useful in terms of bringing specific focus to electronic records issues, and addressing issues that may be generally new or unfamiliar to employees.

4. **Records Hold Policy.** Organizations need a mechanism for informing affected individuals and departments when normal Information Management practices must be suspended because of anticipated or commenced investigations, audits, or litigation. The Records Hold policy and related procedures also may provide forms and other standard documents to be used for the legal, compliance, tax, and/or audit departments to disseminate information on the occasion of a Records Hold.

Create Clear and Unambiguous Directives

Policies and practices do little good if employees cannot understand them, or if the directives are unclear or ambiguous. Particularly where information technology use is being addressed, many organizations seem tempted to use vague language that doesn't require them to investigate all the implications of a policy on the end user or administrator.

Avoid Technology Snafus

The need for clarity is illustrated in the hypothetical case of a medical insurer whose policy states:

> *All business areas may use electronic technologies to manage and store their business content, provided it is done properly and adequately.*

Based on that policy "guidance" from the head office, a regional office moves ahead with plans to purchase and install a large imaging system to convert all existing paper records to electronic form. To save time and bring the project in under budget, they decide that initially, the only *metadata* (data about data) that will be entered about each record in the database for indexing and search purposes is the claim number.

Years and millions of images later, the company is sued by a group of customers, and in the course of the litigation, all documents related to those customers are requested. However, because the company could not search the imaged records by any criteria other than claim number, they are forced to spend tens of thousands of dollars and hundreds of hours manually searching through their database of imaged records to find those responsive to the discovery order.

The company's failure to provide detailed directives on proper indexing of electronic imaged records exposed the company to unnecessary expense. Had the company's imaging experts been consulted by the policy makers, they might have explained how they developed their imaging procedures, which took into consideration such laws as IRS Revenue Procedure Ruling 97-22, which requires "an indexing system for records retrieval." (See Chapter 16 for more information about this IRS rule and its impact on IMC.)

Personal Use of Company Resources

A company has a policy that states:

> *Employees may use company computer resources for personal reasons to the extent such use does not waste company resources, impair system functionality, or impair job performance.*

Mel Brick, a new accountant at the company, decides to download music from his favorite bands using a P2P file sharing program. Having just read the employee manual after he was hired, the company's policy is fresh in his mind, so he is careful to download music only during his lunch break.

Days later, a certified letter from a record industry lawyer arrives, informing the company that it is being sued for infringing on nearly a dozen musicians' intellectual property rights. The company's information security guru seizes Mr. Brick's computer and finds the infringing songs, as well as three pornographic movies that Brick claims he did not download. Also, it becomes clear that Mel has inadvertently provided access to all the files on his computer, including confidential financial information, by tapping into the file sharing network.

Here is clear case of a company failing to provide clear and sufficiently detailed guidance to its employees. Mel Brick thought he was properly interpreting the vague language found in the policy and, coupled with some technological ignorance, he has put the company in jeopardy. Not only is the policy unclear on what activities are permissible, but also it gives no clue as to what is considered a waste of company resources.

Although it is not possible or practical to anticipate all the specific ways that employees may use "company computer resources for personal reasons," organizations do have a responsibility to anticipate the Information Management implications of the technology they provide to employees. In this example, the company should have been aware of the legal and security implications of P2P file sharing over the Internet and specifically have prohibited employees from using this technology through policy.

See Chapter 9 for more information about addressing personal use of organizational resources at work.

Keys to Clarity

Organizations are sometimes under the illusion that broad, vague, or general language will make their policies and procedures more flexible, or give them latitude in the way they enforce them.

However, clear, precise, and unambiguous language protects the organization by limiting interpretation, thus providing greater certainty about the outcome of a dispute. It also minimizes the likelihood of violations in the first place.

In cases where there is ambiguity in the language of a policy and procedure, the courts typically interpret the document in a way that favors the employee, not the employer that drafted the language.

Techniques that organizations can use in drafting clear, unambiguous policies are as follows:

- Use examples and illustrations.
- Be brief and concise. Sometimes the more you try to explain, the more confusing it becomes.
- Separate individual policies and procedures into discrete documents when possible, instead of providing one long, run-on manual that employees are less likely to read through because of the overwhelming length.
- Require employees to sign and "certify" that they have received, read, and understood the policies and procedures given to them. At a minimum, repeat the process whenever major policy changes are made.

Policies in the Real World

When policies and procedures are put to the test in the real world, you can be sure that any weakness in their development, implementation, and enforcement will be exposed and possibly used against you. The case of *Palmer v. Lenfest Group*[1] clearly illustrates this point.

Lenfest, a local cable company, provided free basic and premium cable service to its employees as a job perk. But employees were required to pay 50% for some other services, such as pay-per-view. Some employees who handled customer accounts also had the ability to access their own accounts, but company policy prohibited them from doing so.

The policy prohibiting employees from making changes to their own accounts and related documentation was not included in the employee manual, but instead was e-mailed to company managers to be distributed to the employees who reported to them. In addition, the requirement to pay 50% of pay-per-view services was not in the employee manual or in any written policy, perhaps because the manual and policies had not been updated since the company had introduced pay-per-view technology.

According to the court, Palmer, a dispatcher at Lenfest, failed to pay her $68 cable bill, and her cable service was scheduled for disconnection. Palmer accessed her own account and gave herself a payment extension. When that deadline passed, her cable was automatically disconnected. She once again accessed the system and reversed the disconnection.

When Palmer's unauthorized changes were finally discovered, Palmer was terminated for theft of company property (cable TV services), and a legal dispute over unemployment benefits ensued. Even though the company eventually won the case, a nasty and expensive legal battle that dragged on for months likely could have been avoided if the company had been more vigilant in the way that it implemented and enforced its policies and procedures.

However, in *Allen v. AMTRAK*,[2] the company was able to successfully defend a hostile work environment suit when it promptly disciplined an employee after becoming aware of harassing behavior; when several offensive flyers were posted, it quickly removed the flyers, filed an incident report with police, and held an all-employee meeting to explain that the incident was unacceptable and under investigation, and none of the incidents was repeated. The court observed that any racial harassment violates written policies, and the company had a functioning dispute resolution officer and staff.

In California, employers are liable without fault for acts of employee harassment by a supervisor. However, damages can be reduced if the employee fails to report the incident and the company can establish that by virtue of its functioning, anti-harassment policies and procedures, and record of effective action against complaints, that the employee's failure to report sooner would be unreasonable.[3]

What We Can Learn

- **Keep policies up-to-date**. Policies need to be regularly reviewed and updated. The cable company failed to update its policies to keep pace with technology, which allowed Palmer to argue that she did not have to pay her 50% share for pay-per-view services. In addition, the employee manual did not explicitly state that updates to the manual could be distributed via e-mail, which raised doubt about the legitimacy of the policy sent via e-mail in this case.
- **Don't over-rely on policies**. The case likely would never have happened if employees were not given access to their own accounts. In most technology environments, it would be easy for administrators to use IDs and passwords to restrict access only to authorized employees.
- **Monitor compliance**. Since Palmer accessed her account more than once in violation of policy, a system of compliance monitoring might have detected the violation earlier.

- **Be consistent.** Palmer defended her access and changing of her account by stating: "I've done it before without any ramification and that's why I did not believe there would be any ramifications this time." Employers must consistently follow their own policies in order for them to have value.
- **E-mail must be used carefully for policy notices.** Unlike the paper-based employee manual, which Palmer had signed, there was no easy way to demonstrate that the employee had received, read, and understood the policy sent to her via e-mail. The employer did provide e-mail records that showed that the e-mail had been sent to Palmer, but doubt in this area was a central part of the dispute. There are better digital methods that can be used to show that an employee accessed and even electronically signed a policy. Many companies use their intranet for this purpose, for example. In addition, the decision to send the e-mail first to supervisors, who then had responsibility to send it on to their reports, was not a best practice, as it contributed to creating doubt about whether or not Palmer received the e-mail message containing the policy.

Policies Should Be Technology-Neutral

Information Management policies that address information technology should be "technology-neutral." That is, they should be written in such a way that they would not go out of date when an organization's technology practices change or when new technology is adopted. The vast majority of laws that address information technology take the same approach: by covering broad principles and goals they can stand the test of time while the technology landscape shifts around them.

This is also one of the reasons why statutes are generally broad, whereas the regulations that implement the statutes are more specific, and often do provide specific technical and procedural requirements. In much the same way, it will often be necessary to provide employees with directives and instructions that specifically address the right way to use a particular technology—guidance that will have to be kept up to date if the technology implementation changes. Such directives and instructions support the broader policy. This guidance often takes the form of training materials.

Making company-wide policy is often a laborious and expensive task, so it is a good practice to write policies that remain relevant for the longest period possible. That being said, organizations also have to build a process for periodic review and revision of policies, to accommodate changes in the law, business focus and structure, technology, and so on.

For example, consider the following policy directive:

> *All confidential information must be encrypted before being trans-mitted over the Internet.*

This statement is technology-neutral in two ways. First, it does not specify the technology used to transmit the information over the Internet, so it is "neutral" enough to encompass e-mail, instant messaging, and other digital communications technologies that the company may use now or in the future. Second, it does not stipulate the method of encryption that must be used, which allows the company to employ the best methods and products available at any time.

On the other hand, consider this policy statement:

> *Employees must use the encryption feature of their e-mail program to encrypt all e-mail messages transmitted over the Internet.*

This statement would need to be complemented by other policy and/or procedural statements addressing additional digital communication tools. Also, it would need to be updated if the company changed the method or software program used for encrypting e-mail.

Writing technology-neutral policy statements in the first place can give policies more longevity.

Guiding IT/IS with Policies and Procedures

Your organization's IT/IS department needs to be guided by Information Management policies and procedures when selecting, building, configuring, and maintaining technology. Each choice made by IT staff in these areas can have a major impact on your organization's ability to meet its Information Management goals and obligations.

For example, in 1997, the FDA released 21 CFR Part 11, a regulation that allows the use of electronic records and signatures in the pharmaceutical industry. The purpose of Part 11 was to "permit the widest possible use of electronic technology, compatible with FDA's responsibility to protect the public health."[4]

Part 11 provides detailed requirements for compliant information systems. The impact of these requirements on the selection, creation, configuration, and management of IT systems in the industry is wide-ranging and complex. In fact, the FDA has since released guidance on several occasions specifically designed to help companies understand the implications of the regulation on these activities.[5]

Some of the requirements of Part 11 for compliant IT systems include:

- System validation
- Electronic copies
- Records protection
- System access
- Secure, computer-generated, time-stamped audit trails
- Operational sequencing checks
- Authority checks
- Device checks
- Written policies for signature users
- Documentation controls

The policies and procedures that inform the selection, building, and management of IT systems that comply with these requirements requires a great deal of collaboration among Technology, Legal, Compliance, and other areas of an organization—with the key principle being that the policies drive the technology, and not the other way around.

Organizations also face the choice of buying or building systems that are compliant. As mentioned in Chapter 3, some technology vendors produce "off-the-shelf" software and hardware that is specifically designed to address a variety of compliance needs, such as the storage and management of electronic records in compliance with industry electronic records regulations, such as FDA Part 11, SEC Rule 17a-4, and a variety of related laws and regulations. Many of these products are also designed to integrate with and complement internal solutions that are custom-built to address organizations' unique operating needs. A GRC analysis also informs the decision-making process for compliant information systems. More investment will be directed towards systems which address high areas of risk, possibly justifying additional or custom functionality. On the other hand, areas of low risk may only justify COTS software or hardware.

Resist the Temptation to Make Catch-All Policies

The electronic age has been a boon to the policy drafters. Companies not only need e-mail policies but also e-mail etiquette guidelines, e-mail record retention rules, instant messaging policies, Internet "appropriate use" guidelines, and so on. While there may be lots of policies to draft, when you take on the task of drafting a policy related to Information Management, make sure the scope is clearly defined and that you do not take on too much.

It may be tempting to create an "everything, including the kitchen sink" policy that is designed to cover all your Information Management issues in one shot, but such efforts are usually doomed to failure. Success is much more likely if you start out with a few of the key issues that need to be addressed, cover them in smaller policies, then move on and add to your body of policy over time. Successive policies can be consolidated and revised down the road, if needed.

That being said, it is also important to consult with stakeholders, and sketch out a short-, medium-, and long-term drafting roadmap, taking into consideration high-level policy imperatives before any drafting begins. This will ensure that the overall scope of your Information Management program is broad enough, and there is not a great deal of confusing overlap amongst the various policies that are created along the way.

Address Ongoing Changes in the Law

From time to time, there will be changes in laws and regulations that will require you to change Information Management policies and procedures. For example, consider the case of a multinational company that has an e-mail policy that states:

> *Employees have no right to privacy with respect to e-mail on the company e-mail system, and the company may review, access, or monitor e-mail usage and message content.*

The company has a division in France, where the Social Chamber of the Supreme Court ruled in 2001 that employee e-mail could not be accessed and viewed by an employer, even if the company advised employees that it would do so. On the heels of that ruling, company policy clearly needs to change to reflect the change in law.

However, if the policy had been written as follows, no change would be required and the policy would still work universally throughout the entire organization:

> *The company reserves the right to review, access, monitor, audit, or make available any e-mail messages on the company e-mail system, to the full extent allowed by law.*

Other recent legal changes brought about by new or updated laws and regulations, such as Sarbanes-Oxley, have also required many companies to revisit Information Management policies and procedures. For example, Sarbanes-Oxley lengthens the time that public company auditors need to keep audit work papers—a change that may need to be reflected in up-to-date retention rules.

Addressing Policy Violations: A Four-Stage Program Courtesy of the FTC

Sometimes it's the simplest things that get you in trouble. How many people have typed an e-mail address in the "to" or "cc" box of their e-mail program that they actually meant to put in the "bcc" box—thereby revealing to the recipients exactly who else was getting the same message? For most people, the consequences of this little slip-up are probably minimal—maybe a little embarrassment.

However, when one of the world's largest drug makers makes a similar mistake, it's a different story. In 2002, an FTC investigation revealed that a major pharmaceutical company had sent an e-mail message to nearly 700 Prozac users that unintentionally included each user's e-mail address in plain sight in the e-mail message's "to" field. In other words, 700 people just found out that you use Prozac.

Not only was this embarrassing for the company, but it also violated the trust of its customers, not to mention its own privacy policy.

According to the FTC, the company "failed to maintain or implement internal measures appropriate under the circumstances to protect sensitive consumer information."

In fact, the FTC said that the company failed to:

1. "provide appropriate training for its employees"
2. "provide appropriate oversight and assistance for the employee who sent out the e-mail, who had no prior experience in creating, testing, or implementing the computer program used"
3. "implement appropriate checks and controls on the process."

The FTC also stated that the company also "violated a number of its own written security procedures."

Under the FTC settlement that resulted, the company was required to "establish and maintain a four-stage information security program," which required the company to:

1. Designate appropriate personnel to coordinate and oversee the program.
2. Identify reasonably foreseeable internal and external risks to the security, confidentiality, and integrity of personal information, including any such risks posed by lack of training, and to address these risks in each relevant area of its operations, whether performed by employees or agents, including: (i) management and training of personnel; (ii) information systems for the processing, storage, transmission, or disposal of personal information; and (iii) prevention and response to attacks, intrusions, unauthorized access, or other information systems failures.
3. Conduct an annual written review by qualified persons, within ninety (90) days after the date of service of the order and yearly thereafter, which shall monitor and document compliance with the program, evaluate the program's effectiveness, and recommend changes to it.
4. Adjust the program in light of any findings and recommendations resulting from reviews or ongoing monitoring, and in light of any material changes to [the company's] operations that affect the program. [6]

The FTC's analysis of the problem in this case is instructive. Although it is clearly impossible to prevent employees from making mistakes entirely, it is possible to design and implement Information Management programs that minimize the likelihood of such mistakes occurring—and minimize the magnitude of such mistakes when they do occur. The program outlined by the FTC here also introduces auditing and monitoring principles that will be explored in greater detail in Key 5.

Notes

[1] *Palmer v. Lenfest Group*, 2000 Del. Super. LEXIS 81.

[2] 228 Fed. Appx. 144, 147, 2007 U.S. App. LEXIS 2216 (3d Cir. 2007).

[3] *Myers v. Trendwest Resorts, Inc.*, 148 Cal. App. 4th 1403, 1421, 56 Cal. Rptr. 3d 501, 513 (2007).

[4] "Guidance for Industry, Part 11, Electronic Records; Electronic Signatures—Scope and Application," FDA, February 2003.

[5] See, for example, "Guidance for Industry, Part 11, Electronic Records; Electronic Signatures—Scope and Application," FDA, February 2003.

[6] "Eli Lilly Settles FTC Charges Concerning Security Breach," FTC Press Release, January 18, 2002

9

Information Management Policy Issues

A compliant Information Management program must address myriad policy issues. The intention of this chapter is not, however, to provide a catalogue of those issues. Rather, this chapter focuses on a selection of issues that are worthy of specific focus because they commonly seem to cause problems for organizations, either because of their complexity or their relative newness.

Issue #1: Electronic Discovery

> *In this...era of widely publicized evidence destruction by document shredding, it is well to remind litigants that such conduct will not be tolerated in judicial proceedings. Destruction of evidence cannot be countenanced in a justice system whose goal is to find the truth through honest and orderly production of evidence under established discovery rules.*
>
> *Cabnetware, Inc. v. Sullivan, 1991 U.S. Dist. LEXIS 20329*

Increased reliance on information technology has inevitably led to greater use of electronic evidence in litigation, investigations, audits, and other formal proceedings. In fact, according to the courts, "[c]omputers have become so commonplace that most court battles now involve discovery of some type of computer-stored information."[1] Litigators often take advantage of this lack of preparation by making digital information, especially e-mail, a target of discovery.

Every organization involved in litigation, audits, investigations, and other formal proceedings needs to turn over all relevant information in their "care, custody, or control" to the opposing side (unless subject to a privilege, such as attorney-client), regardless of how embarrassing or damaging it is. Additionally, regulators and auditors may ask for information regarding transactions that occurred years earlier.

What Is Discoverable?

All parties in litigation must disclose "a copy of, or a description by category and location of, all documents, electronically stored information, and tangible things the disclosing party has in its possession, custody or control and may use to support its claims or defenses..."
Federal Rules of Civil Procedure[2]

The *Federal Rules of Civil Procedure*, which provide discovery rules (among other things) for federal courts, define a discoverable "document" as including, "any designated documents or electronically stored information—including writings, drawings, graphs, charts, photographs, sound recordings, images, and other data or data compilations—stored in any medium from which information can be obtained either directly or, if necessary, after translation by the responding party into a reasonably usable form."[3] As this definition of discoverable information is very broad, it could be applied to nearly any type of electronic information imaginable.

Because of the scope of allowable electronic discovery, organizations need to think beyond traditional definitions of an "electronic record" or "document," and consider the entire range of digital information that may be subject to a discovery order. While the need to produce word processing and spreadsheet documents may be obvious to most organizations, e-mail, instant messages, presentations, server log files, HTML code, and other "casual" or "hidden" types of evidence may not be.

An organization's electronic discovery plan should consider the full range of electronic information that the courts may require it to find and produce.

WHAT SECRETS ARE LURKING ON YOUR COMPUTER?

When investigators examine a computer during a trial or other formal proceedings, they can learn a great deal about the owner of the computer from many obscure sources that even the most sophisticated computer user may not think of. From an information security perspective, this also presents challenges when computers are hacked or stolen.

For example, words that a user has added to the custom dictionary in his or her word processing and e-mail programs can reveal a lot about that person's business. A consultant may have added the names of clients, places, and products relating to their work, to avoid the annoyance of a spell-checker consistently tripping over them in word processing documents and e-mail messages. These proper names and confidential data (along with industry jargon) are likely to be extremely important indeed, as they were used frequently enough to cause a spell-checking annoyance.

Electronic Discovery Planning Checklist

To prepare for the possibility of a discovery order covering electronic records, consider the following questions:

1. **Access.** Can electronic records and information be quickly and efficiently found and produced from the storage media and devices upon which they are stored? If not, consider revisiting retention plans, data center capabilities, indexing and searching methods, and characteristics of storage technology in use.

2. **Separation.** If "responsive" e-records (i.e., those relevant to the litigation) will be viewed in electronic form, can they be easily separated from "non-responsive" records and information? This is required to protect against the inadvertent disclosure of irrelevant information that may be proprietary or confidential, and to protect information subject to the attorney-client privilege and/or the attorney work product doctrine. If not, consider how system configuration or new technology investments may provide this functionality, by allowing several different "views" of information according to metadata, access privileges, and other search mechanisms and criteria.

3. **Long-term access.** Can records be preserved in such a way that they can be found, accessed separately, utilized, produced, and/or printed several

years from now if required? Have you accounted for media, software, and hardware obsolescence? These should be standard components of any Information Management program.

4. **Disposition.** Does your organization have outdated, unneeded information and records "lying around" that no longer need to be retained? Ensure that records disposition procedures account for the disposition of *all copies* of digital information.

AN E-DISCOVERY SCENARIO

Your corporate attorney asks you about the company's ability to search for and produce e-mail messages. She needs some help responding to a request from a regulator regarding complaints about aggressive sales tactics targeted at the elderly, and wants to know what e-mail records can be searched and found in the next two weeks.

Are you prepared to respond to her needs? In particular:

- Who would you contact to search and find the required e-mail (called *responsive* e-mail in legal terminology)?
- Do you know for certain what records exist and where to find them?
- Do you have a listing of computer systems, applications, and their administrators and locations within the company?
- Where would you start to look and whom could you assign to help?
- If you have to look in all company facilities in which servers or computers are located, which staffers at each location will do the looking?
- If employees are asked to look through their stored e-mail and for responsive material, how much time will that take, and what will the cost be in terms of lost work, opportunity costs, and real hard costs?
- Which employees could be pulled from their current duties to help search for needed e-mail?
- What contents are stored on backup tapes, and how long are they retained?
- With your company's current technology, can you search every place an e-mail may be stored, and if not, what will you do or whom will you rely upon for assistance?

If you can't readily answer those questions, you should develop a more comprehensive and responsive electronic discovery plan.

The vast majority (89%) of the companies responding to a recent Kahn Consulting survey were actively addressing e-discovery issues. Overall, 93% of organizations were addressing e-discovery, GRC, and/or RIM issues.[4]

Issue #2: Privacy

You've likely received privacy policy statements from your bank, your stock-broker, and your creditors in the past year. And you have probably noticed that e-commerce websites publicize their privacy policies. Whether you've bothered to read any of them or not, you certainly know that privacy has become a prominent consumer issue. The personal information that banks, brokerage firms, creditors, e-merchants, and others collect about their customers is so valuable that other marketers are willing to pay tidy sums for such data. But consumers have become very protective of their private information.

Private Information Is an Asset

Government has recognized the value of private personal information. In *Collier v. Dickenson*,[5] the court ruled that the sale by the Florida Department of Motor Vehicles of the plaintiffs' personal information to mass marketers without the plaintiffs' consent could violate the Driver Privacy Protection Act (DPPA), 18 U.S.C. § 2721-2725, which prohibits disclosure of personal information obtained by the DMV in connection with a person's motor vehicle record without the consent of the person. Plaintiffs could also bring a general civil action for deprivation of rights under 42 U.S.C. § 1983.

Privacy Policy Revisions

Internet retailer Amazon.com faced a similar outcry in 2001 when it alleg-edly made a change to its privacy policy that would allow it to sell its cus-tomer information to a third-party in the event that it was acquired or went out of business. The FTC launched an investigation into the way Amazon.com's change in its privacy policy affected consumers. Around the same time, Amazon paid up to $1.9 million to settle a class action lawsuit launched by users of the company's "Alexa" service, who complained that personally identifiable information was being collected and retained in violation of the company's privacy policy. The FTC said that, "certain of Amazon.com's and Alexa Internet's practices likely were deceptive," and Amazon.com agreed to pay $40 to each affected user.

Organizations must ensure that their privacy policies are comprehensive enough to address all reasonably foreseeable events, like mergers, acquisitions, new business partners, and changes in business direction. Also, organizations must be prepared to live by the promises made in these policies. If drastic changes are required, it may be necessary to "grandfather" existing customers under the old policy, while applying the new policy only to new customers. In any case, a proactive communication plan for all customers should be a prerequisite of any privacy policy change.

Writing a Privacy Policy Is Not Enough

Even the most well drafted policy won't protect the organization if the policy is not implemented. In Illinois, a consumer brought suit against a retailer for intentionally failing to follow policies designed to keep customer's personal information secure after her debit and credit card information kept by the retailer was stolen by a hacker. Under the Illinois Consumer Fraud and Deceptive Practices Act, the practice must inure to the defendant's benefit. The plaintiff solved this problem by alleging that failure to follow the security procedures enabled the defendant to save money.[6]

Ownership of Information

Your organization has a responsibility to properly manage and protect information assets as it would any other asset that it owns. The data stored on the information systems across your organization, from the largest customer relationship management databases to the smallest handheld e-mail devices, are your organization's lifeblood, and must be protected as such.

The information that employees generate in their day-to-day working activities is also part of your organization's information asset collection. It is your responsibility to inform employees, through policies and training, that all such *business information* is the property of the organization. This will help to establish the importance of the information and set expectations for how this information will be treated when an employee leaves your organization.

The following is a sample policy statement that informs employees about this issue.

Ownership of Company Information: Sample Policy Statement

All information that you create, receive, and/or use while conducting company business is owned by the Company, regardless of whether that information is in paper, electronic, or any other tangible form. In addition, all employees must provide all business information in their possession or control to the Company upon request, at any time, for any reason.

Individuals who cease to be employees of the Company must provide original and all copies of any business information to his or her supervisor prior to leaving the company. All business information located in any Company facility or facilities managed by another entity on behalf of the Company are presumed to be company property. All business information created or stored on or in a Company computer, imaging system, communications system, telecommunications system, storage device, storage medium, or any other Company system, medium, or device are presumed to be company property.

All business information, regardless of its location, that in any way pertains to the Company or Company business is presumed to be Company property. Only upon a showing that the business information in question does not in any way relate to Company business will such information be deemed to be other than company property. Theft or appropriation of any business information is strictly prohibited. Giving access to another person who is not authorized to have access to, review, or otherwise see company business information is also strictly prohibited.

Undertaking these prohibited acts may result in termination and/or civil or criminal penalties.

© 2003, 2008, Randolph A. Kahn, ESQ., and Barclay T. Blair. For informational purposes only. Get the advice of counsel before adopting any Information Management policy element.

Privacy of Employee Information at Work

You need to be clear with employees about whether or not they should expect that the information they create and receive on the job is private. Generally speaking, organizations in the United States have taken the approach that such information is not private, and the organization thus reserves the right to access and review it at will.

U.S. courts have generally supported this approach. For example, in *Garrity v. John Hancock Mut. Life Ins. Co.*,[7] two female employees were fired for sending sexually explicit e-mail over the company e-mail system, in contravention of the company e-mail policy. The employees viewed the e-mail containing the offensive content as personal, and argued that the company invaded their privacy when it accessed and examined it. The court weighed the issues in order to determine if "the expectation of privacy was reasonable."

In this case, the court did not find that expectation reasonable, for several reasons:

- The company's e-mail policy stated, "Company management reserves the right to access all Email files," and "there may be business or legal situations that necessitate company review of Email messages and other documents."
- The company "periodically reminded employees that it was their responsibility to know and understand the e-mail policy," and employees had been warned about "several incidents in which employees were disciplined for violations."
- The two employees testified that they sent the e-mail messages (some of which were jokes) to other employees with the expectation that they would subsequently be forwarded to others.
- The employees admitted that they knew the company had the ability to examine company e-mail messages.

Legal opinions on this approach to employee privacy at work are not consistent in every jurisdiction, and companies should investigate the laws of each jurisdiction in which they do business. For example, the Social Chamber of the Supreme Court of France ruled in 2001 that an employee's personal e-mail sent or received on company systems could not be accessed and viewed by an employer, even if the company advised employees that they would do so.

Privacy of Employee Information: Sample Policy Statement

Company resources used by employees to create, transmit, receive, and store business information, such as computers, the email system, and facsimile machines, should only be used for business purposes. In addition, the information in these systems should only be related to Company business. These resources, and the information contained within them, are the property of the Company. Furthermore, the company reserves the right to access and review any business information, whether it is located in company facilities or not.

Employees do not have and should not expect any right to privacy with respect to any Company business information, including email transmission, electronic communication, or Internet or intranet communication. The Company reserves the right to monitor the use of any company property, equipment, phone line, computer, software, or any storage device.

© 2003, 2008 Randolph A. Kahn, ESQ., and Barclay T. Blair. For informational purposes only. Get the advice of counsel before adopting any Information Management policy element.

Issue #3: Protecting Company Information— the Programmer's Toolkit

Computer programmers often make copies of programs they create for their employers for their personal use. They may use the programs as part of their "portfolio," examples of their work they can show other potential employers. They may reuse the code in other projects so that they don't have to reinvent the wheel. For whatever reason, this practice can run up against the employer's desire to maintain the confidentiality of their own proprietary information. By reusing code developed for company A in a project for company B, company B may enjoy the fruits of the programmer's labor for company A from reduced costs in terms of reduced programming time, up to what may be the incorporation of innovative and proprietary functionality developed for company A into company B's products.

In *United States v. Shiah*,[8] the U.S. government attempted to prosecute a former programmer, Shiah, under the Economic Espionage Act (EEA) after the programmer created a toolkit of files developed while employed by one company, Broadcom, and used them for a subsequent employer. The government was able to establish that Shiah had copied the files without authorization, that the files constituted trade secrets as defined in the EEA, and that Shiah knew the information constituted trade secrets. The court found, however, that the measures taken by the company to keep the information secret were "barely sufficient to qualify as reasonable" at the time the misappropriation occurred, in 2003. The court observed that "the reasonableness standard will become more and more stringent as time passes. Over time, there will be and have been improvements in technology, information, and knowledge pertaining to data secrecy, as well as more awareness of the EEA and its implications."

The measures taken by Broadcom appear to be impressive:

> Broadcom's measures included a Confidentiality Agreement signed by every employee. The Confidentiality Agreement explained the value placed on confidentiality at Broadcom and attempted to indicate which documents were considered confidential. This document also prohibited employees from taking confidential information with them upon their departure. Furthermore, Broadcom protected its electronic data through its information technology team, which managed firewalls, file transfer protocols, intrusion detection software, passwords to access the Intranet, a layer of protection between the Intranet and Internet, and selective storage of files. When sharing information with outside entities, Broadcom required non-disclosure agreements, tracked the sharing through DocSafe, and marked documents as confidential. Finally, Broadcom maintained a high security physical facility.

However, the court found a number of deficiencies in Broadcom's efforts. Broadcom failed to thoroughly explain the Confidentiality Agreement to Shiah before he signed it, and failed to give Shiah a copy so that he could refer to it over the course of his employment. Broadcom also did not give Shiah training about what information is confidential and how to handle confidential information. The Agreement was overbroad in that it designated almost all information as confidential, so that it would be difficult for Shiah to determine what information actually was confidential. Ongoing training should have been provided to Shiah and other employees, which should have included methods for ensuring that information stayed protected. Broadcom also lacked a comprehensive system for designating which documents were or were not confidential.

The court also criticized Broadcom's performance during Shiah's exit interview; which the court found was intended more to scare Shiah than inform him as to what his obligations were regarding Broadcom's confidential information. Finally, Broadcom never checked Shiah's computer before he left, which would have revealed that he had recently copied thousands of files from the computer. The government's prosecution of Shiah ultimately failed, however, because it could not prove that Shiah intended, beyond a reasonable doubt, to misappropriate the trade secrets for the economic benefit of anyone other than Broadcom, with the intent or knowledge that Broadcom would be injured.

Lessons Learned

- Make sure that policies regarding confidential information are thoroughly explained to employees when they first begin working for the company, ensure they have a copy of the policies by having them sign an acknowledgment that they have received them (and that the policies have been explained to them, and the employees have had the opportunity to ask questions about them).
- The policies should clearly identify confidential information and contain a process by which employees can easily identify information as confidential.
- Develop policies and procedures for departing employees—policies that establish that the company owns all information stored on company systems, and procedures that minimize the chance that employees will steal information when they leave. The obligations of departing employees regarding confidential information should be clearly explained to them in an unintimidating manner.
- Immediately disable all network and e-mail access when the employee is terminated, or at a predetermined time on the employee's last day. Instruct security personnel to develop procedures for quickly disabling network access for any employee at any time, as instructed by senior

management. Inspect any computers used by employees for work purposes to determine whether any files have been recently copied.

- Use Information Management policies to inform employees that you reserve the right to monitor their use of corporate systems, including the e-mail system.
- Your most valuable information may not be in paper form. Thousands of contacts and volumes of information can fit on a single CD, USB memory stick, mobile e-mail device, and numerous other media that can easily be slipped out of your facilities.

Issue #4: Disaster Recovery and Business Continuance

Although organizations have long prepared contingency plans designed to enable them to survive a disaster, after the events of 9/11, the concept of disaster recovery and business continuance has widened and become more complex. Today, it is clear that disaster recovery and business continuity concepts need to be a part of every Information Management program.

Moreover, contingency plans need to be constantly updated and adapted to account for new realities and risks. For example, when the SEC summarized the "Lessons Learned" by the financial industry after 9/11, they found that, although most Wall Street firms had backup systems and data centers, many had not counted on the "wide-area" disaster of 9/11. As a result, some firms that had "arranged for their backup facilities to be in nearby buildings... lost access to both their primary and backup facilities in the aftermath."[9] Clearly, the events of 9/11 required all firms to revisit many aspects of their disaster recover plans to provide for greater geographic dispersion of backup facilities, and many other elements that respond to newly understood disaster scenarios.

Hurricane Katrina required many firms to put their disaster recovery plans into operation. The importance of following those plans was demonstrated in *Bank of Louisiana v. SunGard Recovery Services, Inc.*[10] The bank had previously tested its disaster recovery plans with SunGard several times, sending backup tapes to SunGard's facility in Georgia and successfully getting their systems running on SunGard's equipment.

When Hurricane Katrina struck Louisiana, the bank's CFO was unable to contact appropriate personnel. Although the CFO contacted SunGard and declared a disaster, she ultimately was not able to find the backup tapes. At SunGard's suggestion, she attempted to start up the system and make a backup using generator power but was not successful. Ultimately, she decided to send the system's hard drives to the vendor to which the bank had previously decided to outsource its IT functions.

The court ultimately found that SunGard had not breached its contract, noting the bank's failure to find the backup tapes, and that the CFO "did not request a deviation in the rehearsed plan. She did not ask SunGard to send personnel or a mobile data center to New Orleans or to deliver the recovery system to a Bank of Louisiana facility."

> There is no evidence that Schaefer [the CFO] consulted with SunGard to notify them she had removed the hard drive or to inquire whether she should send them to Georgia, instead of Michigan, or send the tapes to Georgia after the data was retrieved. Schaefer instead ceased all contact with SunGard until she canceled the disaster declaration on September 14, 2005. Meanwhile, after retrieving the hard drives, she forwarded them to Michigan.

Although the Court lauded the CFO's actions in getting the bank back into operation, nevertheless, it found that SunGard had not breached the contract, and that the bank was liable for the unpaid balance of its 60-month contract.

IMC relies on disaster recovery and business continuance plans that protect business information and records. The best developed and maintained Information Management program is of little utility if the information assets that it is designed to manage are put at risk by an organization's failure to identify and respond to disasters and other risk factors that could cause large-scale loss of data, system outages, and other events that hamper an organization's ability to properly retain and manage business information.

Issue #5: Information Security

Protecting your information assets can be a difficult task, requiring a complex mix of technology, policies, and people to combat expanding threats from viruses to hackers and everything in between. IMC depends on good information security practices, and there are several unique Information Management issues to consider, as explored below.

What Are We Trying to Protect?

There are several reasons why organizations need to implement security strategies for e-mail. Failing to address security around our business information, including e-mail, unnecessarily exposes organizations in all sorts of ways. Information security has a broad purpose that includes:

- Protect information from corruption
- Protect information from misappropriation and misuse
- Protect business operations
- Protect systems from interruptions, failures, and outages, and resulting loss of productivity
- Promote secure business
- Protect company reputation from bad publicity
- Promote confidence in leadership and company management
- Protect the integrity of company data
- Guard against loss or theft of property
- Prevent repudiation and unwinding of business transactions
- Protect the identities of business partners
- Protect different classes of company records, including proprietary, trade secrets, and privileged and confidential communications

Managing Information Security Records

Information security systems create unique types of data that should be given special attention in your Information Management policies and procedures. Some data may require special handling procedures due to their complex or technical nature (e.g., encryption keys), and your Information Management program must account for this type of information. While special procedures may be required, you must ensure that such information is managed according to your established IMC principles, regardless of how unique the content or form of the information may be. You should:

- Conduct an inventory of information security-related software and hardware used throughout your organization, such as encryption systems, firewalls, and user authentication modules.
- Work with IT/IS to determine what kind of information these technologies are generating or storing.
- Determine if any of this information meets your definition of a record. If so, establish a plan for the capture and retention of such information, which may include the creation of new categories for such information in organizational records retention rules.
- Remember that some information (firewall logs in the case of break-in, for example) may be required for litigation and other formal proceedings, and should be included in any Records Hold order related to such proceedings.

A good example of unique information security data is the records created by Public Key Infrastructure (PKI). PKI is a system of policies, people, and technology used to secure information systems. PKI uses advanced cryptography, and can be used for a variety of security-related purposes such as authenticating online identity, and protecting the confidentiality and integrity of information using encryption and digital signatures.

The records produced in the operation of a PKI include a variety of important policies, representations, contracts, and statements that have legal importance to the people and organizations that use and rely on transactions involving PKI. These include documents such as Certification Policies and Certification Practices Statements.

In providing guidance to organizations faced with the task of properly managing PKI records, NARA stated:

> A key premise for this guidance is that PKI-unique administrative records do not constitute a new category of records that require a total "reinvention" of lifecycle Records Management policies and guidance. While the records a PKI produces may be unique in their content and application, the Records Management practices, as already embodied in certain federal statutes, regulations, guidance and standards, still apply.[11]

Road Warriors

Recent surveys indicate that the number of employees who work remotely more than 8 hours per week was about 12 million in 2007, up from 6 million in 2000. The number is expected to hit 14 million by 2009.[12]

Although the benefits of telecommuting includes lower office overhead, improved morale, and boosted productivity,[14] companies must also be careful to consider the Information Management implications of this movement.

Mobile and remote workers present several unique IMC challenges that you must address in policy and procedures, including:

- **Data protection.** Valuable data stored on mobile devices is more vulnerable to theft and loss than those stored inside the walls of the organization. Train employees to be aware that their laptop and PDA are targets for thieves. Airport security screening procedures post-9/11 that require the removal of these devices from carrying bags increase the risk of theft.
- **Retention.** You need a plan to ensure that information on mobile devices is routinely backed up or "synced" to your data center. There are a number of ways to securely perform remote backups to the corporate data center, which you should investigate with your IT/IS department. Data should not be retained or backed up on employees' home computers.
- **Unique records.** Mobile devices may create and retain data in proprietary or obscure formats that may not easily be handled by your Records Management systems. Ensure that data from such devices can be captured and retained in an accurate and reliable fashion before allowing employees to use such devices.

DO YOU HAVE A LAPTOP PROBLEM?

A clothing retailer retained a third-party business to help with hiring employees. A laptop containing the personal information of 800,000 applicants was stolen. According to the September 28, 2007 *Computerworld* story covering the disaster, the company was notifying all that may have been impacted by the data theft and also offering them a year of free credit monitoring and fraud resolution assistance.[15]

DO YOU HAVE A LAPTOP PROBLEM? (*Continued*)

Sales of laptop and notebook computers are outpacing sales of desktop computers.[16] Now is the time to look around your organization and see if you have a laptop problem.

Laptop computers can go anywhere, hold vast amounts of data, and can be connected wirelessly in an increasing number of public places. These advantages can be an Information Management nightmare. Are you addressing these issues?

- Ownership of data on laptop computers, especially if the computers are purchased by employees
- Loss resulting from theft of laptop computer containing proprietary company information
- Remote regular backing up of data for road warriors
- Information security policies for employees connected to public Internet and wireless terminals
- Finding and producing laptop content for litigation, audits, or investigations
- Personal use of laptop computers
- Installing and using only approved software on laptops
- Protection of confidential and trade secret information

Employee Use of Public Terminals

Maybe now you think that equipping employees with the latest and greatest laptops and portable devices isn't the best idea, and you should make road warriors use public Internet terminals like everyone else!

Not quite.

In 2003, a 24-year-old Queens, New York, man pled guilty to federal charges of computer damage, access-device fraud, and software piracy.[17] According to reports, the man had surreptitiously installed keylogging software on a number of Kinko's public Internet access terminals throughout Manhattan. The software enabled him to record each key pressed by customers accessing the Internet, including their passwords and a wealth of confidential and personal information. He then used that information to invade those customer's bank accounts, open new accounts in their names, and transfer funds to unauthorized accounts.

In this case, the hacker's plans seemed limited to using the stolen information to rob personal bank accounts. What if the motives were corporate espionage? What kind of information could he get from a Wall Street administrative assistant checking work e-mail from an Internet café on a lunch break? Financial information? Company passwords? If he or she opened an e-mail attachment containing a confidential presentation, for example, a copy of that file may be created on the public computer, even if the administrative assistant does not save it. And, a sophisticated criminal, such as our man in Queens, would know where to find it.

What can you do to protect against these security risks? One approach is to prohibit employees from using public computers for work purposes. If this is not practical, at a minimum, employees should receive training on the risks of using public terminals.

Patch Management

In the summer of 2003, organizations around the globe were hit with a double whammy. The W32.Blaster computer worm took advantage of operating system security vulnerabilities, and a virulent new form of the Sobig virus generated thousands of infectious e-mail messages. Computers were disabled, airline flights were delayed, and some trains stopped running.[18]

For organizations in the northeastern United States, which were also victims of power outages around the same time, it was an information security "perfect storm." In fact, there is evidence that the worm significantly hampered efforts to address the blackout.[19]

Patch Management (PM) is the art and science of keeping software up to date with the latest *patches*—pieces of computer code that fix a vulnerability, correct mistakes, improve functionality, and so on. While it may sound simple and neat, PM today is messy work. Allowing your antivirus software to automatically update itself on your personal computer is one thing—applying an operating system patch to 20,000 computers across the globe is another.

Organizations employ a variety of tools and techniques to help. For example, many vendors provide software that will automatically inform an IT department when updates are available for a specific piece of software, and then help them test and install that update across an enterprise.

In the case of the W32.Blaster worm, many people questioned why the worm was able to spread at all, given that the vulnerability, and the patch fixing the problem, had been released weeks before. This event served to highlight the many difficulties of PM.

Organizations with massive computer networks that support many different operating systems and complex customized software cannot simply install the latest patch without adequate testing—a process that may take weeks and months to complete. However, new vulnerabilities are discovered every day. According to the CERT Coordination Center (a noncommercial institution that tracks and advises on information security incidents globally), the number of software security vulnerabilities has doubled every year since 1999. In 2002, there were nearly 4,200 reported vulnerabilities.[20]

To address the gap, organizations apply risk management principles, weighing the damage potentially caused by the security vulnerability against the cost of testing and applying the patch. And to ease the pain of applying the patch, many organizations also employ change management techniques to ensure that their systems will not malfunction due to software changes caused by new patches.

Aside from the inherent difficulties of PM, many organizations continue to be vulnerable simply because they have inadequate policies and procedures. Through lack of awareness, commitment, resources, or other reasons, increasingly, organizations without a PM plan are putting themselves, and other organizations, at risk.

Patch Management must be a part of your organization's Information Management Program.

Notes

[1] *Bills v. Kennecott Corp.*, 108 F.R.D. 459, 462 (D. Utah 1985).

[2] Fed. R. Civ. Proc. 26(a)(1)(A)(ii).

[3] Fed. R. Civ. Proc. 34(a)(1)(A).

[4] *"GRC, E-Discovery, and RIM: State of the Industry*—A Kahn Consulting, Inc. Survey in association with ARMA International, BNA Digital Discovery and E-Evidence, Business Trends Quarterly, and the Society of Corporate Compliance & Ethics," (Fall 2008), p. 5, found at http://www. kahnconsultinginc.com/library/surveys.html

[5] 477 F.2d 1306 (11th Cir. 2007), *cert. den.* 128 S.Ct. 869 (2008).

[6] *Richardson v. DSW, Inc.*, 2006 U.S. Dist. LEXIS 1840 (N.D. Ill. Jan. 18, 2006).

[7] *Garrity v. John Hancock Mut. Life Ins. Co.*, 146 Lab. Cas. (CCH).

[8] *United States v. Shiah*, 2008 U.S. Dist. LEXIS 11973 (C.D. Cal. Feb. 19, 2008).

[9] "Summary of 'Lessons Learned' from Events of September 11 and Implications for Business Continuity," Securities and Exchange Commission, February 13, 2002.

[10] *Bank of Louisiana v. SunGard Recovery Services, Inc.*, 2008 U.S. Dist. LEXIS 20788 (E.D. La. Mar. 17, 2008).

[11] "Records Management Guidance For PKI-Unique Administrative Records," National Archives and Records Administration, March 14, 2003.

[12] Eve Tahmincioglu, "The quiet revolution: telecommuting," msnbc.com, October 5, 2007; available at http://www.msnbc.msn.com/id/20281475

[13] "Hotspots: Hot Wireless Initiative," Yankee Group and Gartner Dataquest reports, eMarketer, July 8, 2003.

[14] "Business Benefits of Telecommuting," Economist Intelligence Unit report, eMarketer, July 17, 2003.

[15] Brian Fonseca, "Personal data on 800,000 Gap job applicants exposed in laptop theft," *Computerworld*, September 28, 2007.

[16] "Notebooks Claim Over 50% of Retail PC Sales," NPD Group report, eMarketer, July 9, 2003.

[17] "Queens Man Pleads Guilty to Federal Charges of Computer Damage, Access Device Fraud and Software Piracy," U.S. Department of Justice press release, July 11, 2003.

[18] Guth, Robert A., and Daniel Machalaba, "Computer Viruses Disrupt Railroad and Air Traffic," *The Wall Street Journal*, August 21, 2003.

[19] Verton, Dan, "Blaster Worm Linked to Severity of Blackout," *Computerworld*, September 1, 2003.

[20] CERT website—http://www.cert.org/stats/

Key #2

Executive-Level Program Responsibility

Senior executives and managers must take overall responsibility for the Information Management program.

Key Overview

The success of any important organizational activity depends in large part on the commitment of the organization's senior management team. This commitment can be expressed in concrete ways, such as funding levels; and less tangible ways, such as making it a priority at the executive round table.

IMC is no different. A successful Information Management program requires senior executives and managers to step up and take responsibility for the program's development, implementation, and ongoing improvement.

10

Executive Leadership, *Sine Qua Non*[1]

IMC depends on executives and senior management taking responsibility for their organization's Information Management activities. Executive responsibility is more than just "optics" or keeping up appearances. Rather, as outlined in the *Federal Sentencing Guidelines*, high-level personnel in the organization "must have been assigned overall responsibility to oversee compliance with… standards and procedures." There are many reasons why executive involvement and responsibility is important for IMC, as this chapter explores.

Policy Comes from Above

Senior management is responsible for setting an organization's direction and communicating priorities to employees. High-level, visible executive involvement and responsibility makes clear that IMC is a priority for the organization and is central to its success. Practically speaking, without high-level involvement, employees across the organization may fail to take the initiative as seriously as they should, or they may ignore it altogether.

Policy direction must come from above to achieve the following objectives:

- **Consistency.** To create organization-wide consistency.
- **Resource allocation.** Business units will be reluctant to spend money complying with policy that is not tied directly to their budgets and management objectives unless the policy comes from the top.
- **Motivation.** Employees and managers are motivated to follow the directives of those who evaluate them, so unless the directives come from the top, only pockets of the organization may be motivated to follow the policies. Policy does not come from below.

- **Delegation.** Middle management is most effective at directing implementation, training, and enforcement tasks, not originating policy. Plus, there is little incentive for employees to listen to managers from outside their business group.
- **Influence.** Employees are less likely to listen to designated "policy makers" who lack sufficient authority to impose the change on the organization.
- **Accountability.** In the wake of corporate reform movements and laws like Sarbanes-Oxley, shareholders, boards, and auditors (and regulators in the case of government agencies) are looking to top management for assurances that information is being properly managed. Only the involvement of senior executives can provide this assurance.

Many Information Management initiatives fail for the simple reason that they were being advanced by personnel who did not have, or were perceived not to have, the support or authority of top management.

SENIOR MANAGEMENT'S RESPONSIBILITY

Senior management cannot evade responsibility for recordkeeping practices by sheer ignorance. In *Pastorello v. New York*,[2] the associate director for risk management for a New York hospital pleaded ignorance of the hospital's recordkeeping procedures. In finding the hospital grossly negligent for the loss of key records, the court found that "it was her duty to undertake with some degree of care the process of discovering the existence of such record-keeping procedures." It concluded that "'Defendants' ignorance of their own reporting and record-keeping procedures is not only insufficient to disavow culpability, it is in and of itself culpable."

Companies and Executives Pay the Price for Their Failures

The CEO and other senior executives are ultimately responsible for their organization's performance. In the case of a public company that can be measured by stock performance—if the stock is not performing, heads may begin to roll.

The first few years of this new millennium have illustrated time and again that a failure to properly manage records and information can have disastrous consequences—including a direct impact a company's stock price. For example, reports of an FDA investigation into "fraudulent recordkeeping" at one of the world's largest pharmaceutical companies sent its shares to their lowest point in 12 months.[3]

In the last five years, Records Management, information security, disaster recovery, and a whole host of Information Management issues have been tied directly to a company's performance in the market.

Who Has Time for It?

The average worker today is increasingly being asked to do more. According to the International Labor Institute, 80% of American men and 64% of women now work overtime hours.[4] The pressures of productivity coupled with the rapid pace of technological and economic change mean that employees have less and less time for "non-core" activities (activities that are not directly related to their performance evaluation and compensation).

Unless senior management creates a culture that makes Information Management activities a core responsibility, employees have little practical incentive to take their responsibilities seriously. Employees have enough to do without worrying about activities that are perceived as "nice to have" as opposed to essential.

Organizational Culture

The so-called "star CEO" has taken a bit of a beating lately, with all the reports of excessive compensation packages and corruption coming out of the 1990s boom era and beyond. Still, the CEOs of many of our largest organizations are well-known public figures. And each CEO has a personality that is often reflected in the culture of his or her company.

Indeed, senior management is largely responsible for creating the culture and personality of an organization. If senior management is not shaping the personality of an organization, they are not doing their jobs.

Management shapes an organization's personality by the ethics, values, priorities, and strategies that they lay out and promote in both conceptual and practical ways. For example, a culture of "employee flexibility" may be supported by job sharing, flexible hours, and onsite daycare. A culture of organizational accountability, transparency, and IMC must similarly be supported in real and practical ways: by statements of support from the top; by clear, accessible policies and procedures; by employee training; and by adequate funding.

In short, creating an organizational culture that considers Information Management a normal part of day-to-day business operations and part of every employee's job description is the responsibility of senior management.

It's Not Just the CFO

When companies are prosecuted for financial manipulation and fraud, it is not just the CFO who is targeted. Other members of the executive roundtable are often involved as well. For example, when the SEC brought action against a manufacturer for manipulating its financials, the VP of finance as well as director and member of the audit committee, and the chief operating officer were all charged with violations of securities laws. Many types of fraud and manipulation require the involvement of various parts of the business, such as this one, which involved booking revenue for goods that were not yet shipped, among other things.[5] Everyone at the executive table shares management responsibility for Information Management.

> **EXECUTIVE RESPONSIBILITY FOR PRESERVATION OF EVIDENCE**
>
> In re Prudential Ins. Co. of America Sales Practices Litigation,[6] Prudential was fined $1 million for a failure to preserve evidence relevant to the case, and the court squarely placed the blame on the shoulders of senior management.
>
> Here are some excerpts from the decision:
>
> "Prudential top management...recognized that the sales practices lawsuits and regulatory investigations are an extremely important part of Prudential's business...more importantly, they all recognized Prudential's obligation to preserve documents in connection with the lawsuits and investigations. Yet, none took an active role in formulating, implementing, communicating, or conducting a document retention policy."
>
> *Continues*

EXECUTIVE RESPONSIBILITY FOR PRESERVATION OF EVIDENCE
(Continued)

"When the [preservation order] was entered, it became the obligation of senior management to initiate a comprehensive document preservation plan and to distribute it to all employees." What are the actions senior management must take? Making the attorneys responsible for finding and preserving evidence will not meet the company's obligations. In *Larsen v. Bank One Corp.*[7] the court held that the corporation "must creat[e] a comprehensive document retention policy that will ensure that relevant documents are retained,...and...disseminat[e] that policy to its employees...In addition, the document policy must contain enough specificity to the litigation, or scope, to ensure that relevant documents are preserved." The court scrutinized the policies provided to it carefully, and found them wanting. The court observed that dates on several pages of the policies were after the date of filing of the litigation, and some pages were labeled "proposed." There was also insufficient guidance for employees to determine which documents should be retained for the lawsuit. Furthermore, the court found "scant evidence" that the policies were properly disseminated to employees; noting that some employees were unaware that certain categories of documents had to be preserved. The court found the conduct of the corporation to be sanctionable, permitting several damaging instructions to be given to the jury.

The buck stopped with the head of the company in *3M v. Kanbar.*[8] In that case, the company counsel realized, during a deposition, that a certain e-mail had not been produced to the other side. Counsel's explanation for the problem was that it was necessary to search for the e-mails manually. Rather than compelling the company to perform another manual search, the court ordered the head of the company (and the company itself) to certify that all relevant information had been produced and detail the steps taken to ensure complete production. Although the failure to produce the e-mail was arguably counsel's fault, the court stated, "Given the concern over the previous omission, Defendant(s) would do well to ensure that all responsive documents have been produced before signing."

Fighting the Tide Is a Job for Someone Strong

Too few companies consider the IMC implications of new technology before they implement the technology. As a result, too many organizations have suffered damage that resulted from improper employee use or abuse of information systems. Efforts to address Information Management problems too often only occur reactively, after the damage has been done.

Instead, IMC should be a proactive effort that identifies and addresses problems before they occur—an approach that is likely to be less expensive and more effective in the long run. Only senior management can create the organizational culture that will ensure that a proactive approach is taken.

Before implementing new technology, senior management should ensure that the organization has asked the right questions. These questions include:

- What are the risks of using and misusing the technology?
- What is the likelihood that employees will misuse the technology?
- What is the potential harm to the company if they do misuse the technology?
- Are there any regulatory directives to manage the technology or its output (information, data, or records)?
- Should the company retain the information, data, or e-record from the system for any business, operational, or administrative purposes?
- What can the company do to minimize misuse and liability?
- Do we have policies that tell employees what to do and what not to do?
- Do we have procedures that deal with the details of retention and storage?
- What senior executive will "own" the process of informing employees about the rules and what is expected of them?
- Who will write rules, and how will the policy be disseminated?
- Who will train the employees?
- Who will audit the system?
- Who will discipline the offenders?

Consistency across Lines-of-Business

Having the highest level of management make clear that IMC is a priority throughout the entire organization is imperative to ensure that all business units take action in a uniform and timely manner. Because in many organizations business units are semi-autonomous, direction must come from the very top in order to create consistency across all the units. Directives from peer business units are less likely to be successful.

Kahn Consulting recently worked with a client that took this approach to the implementation of a comprehensive Records Management initiative. The initiative became one of the CEO's main objectives. The project manager sat down with all of the vice presidents and received their buy-in for the project. The company's financial commitment to the project was demonstrated by a budgetary increase of over one and one-half times over a year and a half's time. An atmosphere of ongoing communication was emphasized, and the project team worked closely with the business units. The project produced tangible improvements that were well-received by the vice presidents.

INFORMATION MANAGEMENT VENDOR CHOICES

Employees may think that they have done their organization a service by negotiating a "cheap" deal with an Information Management vendor. However, executives should understand that "cheap" might be "expensive."

A bad vendor choice hampered the plaintiff in *PSEG Power New York, Inc. v. Alberici Constructors, Inc.*[9] The attachments to over 3,000 e-mails became separated from the e-mails due to incompatibility between the discovery vendor's software and the plaintiff's e-mail system. The court required the plaintiff to pay for the reproduction of the data. This was the lesser of two evils for the plaintiff, who did not want to provide the defendant with Outlook .PST files that contained many confidential communications.

Executives must set the tone (as well as the example) for employees who have responsibility for negotiating deals with vendors where Information Management is at stake. That is, skimping on the quality of the service to save pennies today could cost the company dearly tomorrow.

Put Your Money Where Your Mouth Is

IMC is an enterprise-wide effort, one that affects all business units individually and collectively. Overall responsibility for ensuring that these efforts are adequately funded and staffed resides with senior management.

A failure to adequately fund an Information Management program will not only contribute to its demise but will also send the message to employees, board members, and shareholders that the organization does not take Information Management seriously.

Giving a peer business unit responsibility for the Information Management program across the organization is typically a recipe for disaster, as these units do not have control of the budget—which makes it difficult to exercise any real control or to influence the process.

THE ECONOMICS OF TOP-LEVEL COORDINATION

Top-level coordination encourages efficient use of resources and eliminates duplication of effort and technology resources. It would clearly be inefficient, for example, for each business unit in an organization to license and operate a different document management or e-mail system.

Consider the following example: The IT department of a company, without consulting the CIO, purchased a document management application for the entire enterprise. As it turned out, the application failed to address the needs of one particular business unit. So the company had to invest in a separate application to provide that single business unit the functionality it needed. The total cost for the two applications was nearly double the cost of the first application. If the executives of all the business units had been engaged in the original procurement process, the application could have been designed to serve all business units, for not much more cost than the original application.

Uniform technology implementation encourages consistency and efficiency; volume buying also results in better pricing.

Having CIO "oversight" of purchasing and implementation issues helps to ensure that technology will be uniform across disparate business units, which also can increase the success of an Information Management program.

Can the CEO Really Be Held Accountable for Information Management?

The chief executive of an organization bears ultimate responsibility for IMC and may be held accountable by the courts. This was illustrated clearly in *Danis v. USN Communications*,[10] a shareholder class action suit that addressed senior management's failure to properly manage information prior to and during litigation. The company mismanaged records and improperly destroyed information, putting the court in the position of determining which individuals were to blame.

The court found that the CEO:

1. As "head of day-to-day management…had the **authority** and **responsibility** to implement a suitable document preservation program"
2. "Was at fault for **delegating** that function to a person who **lacked** the experience to perform that job properly"
3. "Further was at fault for **failing** to exercise any ongoing **oversight** to ensure that the job was done properly" [emphasis added throughout]

As a result, the court fined the CEO $10,000 to "impress upon [him] the seriousness of the duty of preservation, and to deter others from failing to properly discharge that duty."

This case is a great example for all organizations to study, as it provides insight into the type of expectations that the law has regarding the Information Management responsibilities not only of CEOs but also of boards and middle management.

Specific Issues for the CEO

The court in *Danis* went on to detail its view of how the CEO and the management team failed in its Information Management obligations as follows:

1. **No active management.** The CEO "personally took no affirmative steps to ensure that the [document retention] directive was followed."
2. **No preservation policy.** He did not direct that the company "implement a written, comprehensive document preservation policy, either in general or with specific reference to the lawsuit."

3. **No notice of the need to suspend normal policies.** "He did not instruct that any e-mail or other written communication be sent to staff to ensure that they were aware of the lawsuit and the need to preserve documents."

4. **No supervision.** He "did not meet with the department heads after this staff meeting to follow up to see what they had done to implement the document preservation directive."

5. **Improper delegation.** He "exhibited extraordinarily poor judgment" by delegating these responsibilities to an in-house attorney with no litigation experience nor experience in developing a retention program, especially when he had the option of using an outside law firm with deep experience in these issues. Delegation is covered in detail in Chapter 13.

In-House Council's Responsibility

The CEO was not the only one blamed by the court for the company's Information Management failures. The in-house attorney was criticized because:

1. **No employee notice.** He did "nothing to ensure that all...employees who handled documents that might be discoverable were aware of the lawsuit and the need to preserve documents."

2. **No employee meetings.** He "held no meetings with employees below the managerial level."

3. **No written communication.** He "did not issue any written communications to anyone on the subject."

4. **No supervisory follow-up.** He "did nothing to determine whether the managers who attended the staff meeting followed his direction of communicating to their respective departments the need to preserve documents."

5. **No policy review.** He "did not review the preexisting practices...relating to document preservation for terminated employees and closed offices, to determine whether these practices were still suitable in light of the need to preserve documents as a result of litigation."

The Role of the Board

Even the company's board did not escape blame from the court for the company's Information Management failures. The court faulted the company's board of directors for not taking "any active role in implementing a broader preservation policy," and for not following up with the CEO "to determine if their directive had been implemented."

The court in *Danis* went even further, criticizing the "hands-off" approach of the board:

> The outside directors believed that taking an active role in ensuring preservation of documents was not part of their "responsibility as director[s]," but that "[t]he people down in the trenches who gathered the data" would perform that task. This myopic view begs the question of who was supposed to see to it that the "people down in the trenches" actually carried out the task.

In the wake of Sarbanes-Oxley, it is even riskier for a board to take such an approach today.

EXECUTIVE CHECKLIST

- Routinely and outwardly support the Information Management initiative.
- Clarify your expectations.
- Delegate important tasks to the right senior people. Clarify who should take responsibility for the success of specific initiatives.
- Document your support of Information Management program through presentations, memos, e-mail, voicemail "blasts," webcasts, and the like.
- Adequately fund Information Management initiatives.
- Make clear that Information Management directives apply to, and affect the performance of, all employees and all business units.

Notes

[1] *Sine Qua Non*: an absolute prerequisite.

[2] 2003 U.S. Dist. LEXIS 5231 (S.D.N.Y. Apr. 1, 2003).

[3] "Johnson & Johnson Faces FDA Probe," *Washington Post*, July 19, 2002.

[4] "Overtime and the American Worker," a study by Cornell University Institute for Workplace Studies, 1999.

[5] *SEC v. Lawrence O'Shaughnessy*, Gary H. Klein, Gary K. Levi and Mark Tucker, Civil Action No. 03 CV 3022 (RMB), April 30, 2003.

[6] In re Prudential Ins. Co. of America Sales Practices Litigation, 169 F.R.D. 598 (D.N.J. 1997).

[7] 2005 U.S. Dist. LEXIS 42131 (N.D. Ill. Aug. 18, 2005).

[8] *3M v. Kanbar*, 2007 U.S. Dist. LEXIS 78374 (N.D. Cal. Oct. 10, 2007).

[9] 2007 U.S. Dist. LEXIS 66767 (N.D.N.Y. Sept. 7, 2007).

[10] *Danis v. USN Communications, Inc.* 2000 WL 1694325, N.D.Ill., 2000.

11 What Executive Responsibility Means

In the previous chapter, we examined why executive leadership and responsibility is so critical to the success of compliant Information Management programs. In this chapter we will discuss practical ways in which executives can exercise this leadership role.

Creating a Culture of Information Management Awareness

There are several things that senior executives can do to get the message across to all employees that IMC is important to the organization, is a core part if its day-to-day operations, and is central to its success.

The CEO Statement

Many organizations include a statement or introductory letter from the CEO, chief operating officer, or other high-level executive, as part of the new employee orientation manual provided to employees. This statement may also introduce a Records Management policy, appear on the intranet site that houses Information Management policies and procedures, and be inserted in an e-mail reminder. Whatever the vehicle, it is important that the employee gets the message from an executive.

Although the text of such a statement will naturally vary from organization to organization, its basic elements are:

1. Records and information are valuable assets that the company relies upon for a variety of business and legal purposes.

2. Properly managing information is central to the organization's success.

3. The Information Management program is designed to ensure that this information is available when the company needs it.

4. The company complies with all laws and regulations regarding records and information.

5. It is each employee's responsibility to assist in ensuring that information is properly managed.

6. Failure to comply with Information Management policies and procedures will not be tolerated in any employee or executive.

A SAMPLE CEO STATEMENT

Dear Associates,

As you may already know, our company generates a great deal of information. In fact, we generate and use so much information each day that you could say that information is the lifeblood of our business. Each day, for example, our company generates about 100,000 e-mail messages, and creates more than 50,000 MB of digital information. This is in addition to the thousands of paper documents that we receive and process.

Much of this information has business, operational, legal, and historical importance and therefore must be properly managed. This is a responsibility that we all share. We depend on this information to better serve our customers, to plan and forecast, and to meet our legal and regulatory obligations. Managing this information effectively is central to our success; failing to manage it can result in severe penalties, reduced profitability, and disciplinary action.

All of us are responsible for helping to manage and protect our valuable business information, and to dispose of it only when directed in accordance with written policy. This is why we have created our *Records Management Manual* and its related policies—to ensure that we all understand how to properly manage and use that information throughout our organization.

Regards,

The CEO

The Executive Information Management Council

Once senior management has decided to make IMC a high priority, the next logical step is to turn over execution of the program to an experienced group of senior personnel. It is critical that this group, which makes things happen on a day-to-day basis, be assembled with care. As the *Danis* case, discussed earlier in Chapter 10, makes clear, the court will not tolerate delegation of important activities to unqualified individuals. In addition, Information Management is a multidisciplinary activity that requires the right mix of people and expertise to ensure full compliance.

The precise makeup and responsibilities of this group will vary by organization, but many organizations may want to create an Executive Information Management Council. This Council would have organization-wide responsibility for ensuring that the Information Management program is properly implemented throughout the company, and that needed policies and procedures are in place to address operational, legal, and technical needs and requirements.

The Council might include representatives from the following departments:

- Legal
- Human Resources
- Information Technology
- Finance
- Records Management
- Business Risk Management
- Tax and Audit
- Compliance
- Leadership from affected business units

It may also be helpful to provide a mechanism for "end-user" input. The Council should have the ability to create subordinate committees to address specific Information Management issues at a top level of the organization, and also to coordinate with similar councils within business units. Other considerations in forming the Council include:

- **Size.** The Council members should represent a broad cross-section of the company, to ensure that the concerns of all business units are considered, but small enough to get the job done in an efficient and timely way, without getting bogged down in bureaucratic minutiae.

- **Authority.** The Council should be granted enough authority to make things happen.
- **Charter.** The Council's activities and mandate should be broad enough to ensure that all major issues are addressed but defined narrowly enough that it can address real, practical issues.

What Happens to Records When Executives Leave the Organization?

Organizations must ensure that they retrieve all information and records from departing employees. This is especially important with executives and senior management, who often have the organization's "keys to the kingdom" in their possession, whether in paper files or on their computers. Aside from confidentiality, privacy, privilege, trade secret, and other issues, organizations may need information held by executives to defend the organization in court and to respond to investigations and audits.

In the case of *United States v. Bedell*,[1] the court found where the custodian of an organization is currently employed by that organization, they have no Fifth Amendment privilege to refuse production of those records on the grounds that the act of production would tend to incriminate the custodian. However, where the employee ceases to be employed by the organization, the employee or agency relationship terminates so that the employee is no longer an agent of the corporation and is also not a custodian of the organization's records. Therefore, "when such an individual produces records in his possession he cannot be acting in anything other than his personal capacity," and can exercise their Fifth Amendment right against self-incrimination.

In other cases, such as *Gloves, Inc. v. Berger*,[2] the law has been interpreted differently. In this case, the court found that a custodian of corporate records continues to hold them in his or her capacity as a former representative of the organization, not in a personal capacity, "thus, production of such documents is required regardless of whether the custodian is still associated with the corporation." Other cases have come to similar conclusions.

Many of these problems can be avoided if organizations implement and consistently enforce a clear policy that requires all records in "the possession, custody, or control" of executives to be returned to the organization before the executive's employment is terminated. In the case of executives, companies should consider making this part of a standard employment contract.

WHAT IS GOVERNANCE, RISK AND COMPLIANCE (GRC)?

By Andrew M. Cohen, Esq., Associate General Counsel and VP, Compliance Solutions, EMC Corporation (Used by permission.)

The phrase "Governance, Risk and Compliance" or "GRC" is a common catch phrase with corporations, analysts, technology vendors and consultants. It is often used in the context of organizational struggles to meet legal obligations associated with information management. But what does GRC really mean?

"GRC" is a complicated concept because it encompasses such a broad scope. Take just the "C" in GRC. Compliance can involve everything from the rules for electing members of a corporate board of directors, to how executive compensation is derived and reported, to financial audits, to integrity training, to data collection and preservation for lawsuits, to protection of the environment, and much more. Many analysts, vendors and customers (across disparate functions such as Legal, Finance, HR, Compliance and IT) struggle to define what they mean by "compliance". Indeed, different groups within the same organization may define it in completely different ways.

Similarly, the term "GRC" has some historic baggage because of the way the term has been used by vendors and analysts. For example, some analysts apply the term "GRC" to refer exclusively to workflow tools that track compliance with the Sarbanes Oxley law, others use "GRC" to mean only those products that monitor and log IT system activities, and so on.

GRC: The Process of Setting Information Policies

GRC is a way of understanding how organizations, and departments within them, assess risks, determine priorities, allocate assets and investments, and ultimately set policy. It is helpful to start by breaking down and defining the elements of GRC.

Governance is the act or process of setting policy for an organization.

Risk management is a disciplined way to address uncertainty, to allocate resources, and to balance risk and opportunity based on organizational goals and tolerance for risk.

Compliance is the act or process of adhering to those policies and being able to prove it.

Continues

WHAT IS GOVERNANCE, RISK AND COMPLIANCE (GRC)? *(Continued)*

The set of activities reflected in the term "GRC" is typically implemented by a management team with a charter to set policy ("governance"), assess risk and determine priorities (because there will never be enough resources to do everything, risk cannot be eliminated and it must be embraced to achieve business goals) ("risk"), and to ensure the organization's policies are understood, followed and enforced ("compliance").

"Corporate governance" refers to the way that public corporations are run. It typically includes "governance structures" that set the policies (such as a Board of Directors to represent the interests of shareholders, and executive committees to set the strategy and run the business). It often also includes a mission statement and supporting ethics training and communications to set a cultural tone (so that employees within the corporation will be more likely to act within the policies even when they don't know precisely what all the policies say).

Since information is so critical to every organization, GRC processes are often applied at the corporate level to seek to maximize the value of information, and minimize its costs and risks. Many organizations have begun setting up cross-functional committees of executives (often the General Counsel, Chief Information Officer, Chief Financial Officer, and others) who are tasked with assessing key security, compliance and information management opportunities and challenges. These compliance committees often assess a range of information management choices, triage based on which categories of information are the most critical and the most sensitive, and then sponsor information management and protection projects based on business priorities, and return on investment ("ROI") justifications.

For example, a "Corporate GRC" process may lead to a policy decision that the personally identifiable information ("PII") of a company's customers—such as names, addresses, account numbers, Social Security numbers and the like—must be segregated, securely managed, and that certain statutory obligations to protect such information must be met or exceeded. This policy decision might be driven by a combination of legal requirements, the desire to reduce public relations risk, the opportunity and differentiation created by offering privacy protections to customers that are superior to the competition, and an organizational desire to do the right thing.

Continues

WHAT IS GOVERNANCE, RISK AND COMPLIANCE (GRC)? *(Continued)*

The IT department typically has responsibility to implement many of the information policies set through corporate GRC processes. IT also has its own charter to properly manage the information infrastructure. In the example above, a set of "IT GRC" policies and supporting processes might be applied to help implement the "Corporate GRC" policy. Thus, a corporate policy ("secure the PII and meet or exceed applicable regulatory requirements"), results in a series of IT implementation policies (e.g. "access to customer systems and applications containing PII will be strictly limited, multifactor authentication will be required, PII content will be automatically encrypted", and so on).

Conclusion

Despite some of the confusion about the meaning of GRC, it is a powerful concept because it captures and summarizes a reality about how organizations set priorities, manage risks, allocate assets and set policy, including information management policy. The term GRC is best understood when each of its elements is broken down (G, R and C), when the domain to which a policy is being applied is articulated (e.g., information), and where there is an understanding of the organizational context (e.g. "corporate", "IT" or other company department).

Three quarters of the respondents in the recent Kahn Consulting survey on GRC, RIM, and E-Discovery viewed GRC positively. A majority described GRC as a valuable concept that represents the future of how governance, risk management, and compliance will be addressed by most organizations. When asked about the relationship between GRC and RIM, participants stating that RIM should be an integral part of GRC outnumbered those who felt that the programs should be separate by more than two to one. GRC as a methodology is here to stay.[3]

Notes

[1] *United States v. Bedell*, 2006 U.S. Dist. LEXIS 87212 (E.D.N.Y. Oct. 30, 2006).

[2] *Gloves, Inc. v. Berger*, 198 F.R.D. 6.

[3] "GRC, E-Discovery, and RIM: State of the Industry—A Kahn Consulting, Inc. Survey in association with ARMA International, BNA Digital Discovery and E-Evidence, Business Trends Quarterly, and the Society of Corporate Compliance & Ethics," (Fall 2008), p. 7, found at http://www.kahnconsultinginc.com/library/surveys.html

12 IT Leadership

As the visibility of compliance continues to rise, there is a concurrent increase in the importance placed on information technology and the role of the CIO. Like other parts of the enterprise responsible for risk and compliance, IT's mandate has expanded in the post-Sarbanes-Oxley (SOX) environment. Beyond the traditional charge that comprises the fundamentals of keeping the lights on and the company out of trouble, IT and the CIO now share responsibility for making the business better. Ironically enough, one of the most "siloed" of functions has become one of the most well-positioned to do just that.

CIO.com, January, 2008[1]

In the wake of recent laws and regulations aimed at corporate reform and accountability, such as the Sarbanes-Oxley Act of 2002, chief information officers (CIOs) and their departments are taking responsibility for not only their organizations' technology systems but also for the information stored within those systems. Some view this as an inevitable evolution: it only makes sense that those who "own" the IT systems would be the best people to take responsibility for their contents. To others, the evolution is not so clear and they see trouble ahead.

What is clear is that business and IT executives often see the world very differently. For example, a recent survey by *The Economist* found that although alignment between business and IT leaders had improved over the previous three years, there is still a significant difference of opinion between the two areas over the extent of the alignment. Sixty-one percent of IT executives rated their operations as "well" or "perfectly" aligned, while only 47% of non-IT executive respondents agreed.[2] Which executive knows the real story?

Internal confusion and a lack of communication at the executive level do not bode well.

In many ways, Sarbanes-Oxley is the perfect illustration of the way that IT and business executives may be forced together in ways never imagined before. The law, with its focus on "internal controls" designed to guarantee the accuracy of financial information, among other things, is in many ways a "shotgun marriage" between technological and management controls. As a result, if the CIO didn't already have a seat at the table, in an increasing number of organizations you can be sure that he or she will.

IT Leadership Is Changing

The role of CIOs and other IT executives is changing (or should be changing) in many organizations to reflect our increasing reliance upon digital information for business purposes, and for transactions that have profound legal and regulatory ramifications. The popular view of IT as a service bureau that offers "commodity" information services to the rest of the company is too limited when one considers the staggering growth of technologies like e-mail. Analysts estimate that a typical corporate e-mail account receives about 18 MB of data per day and that this number is expected to grow to over 28 MB by 2011 as both the volume and size of e-mails explode.[3] Much of that daily 18 MB has real business, operational, legal, regulatory, and/or historical significance and must be retained and managed properly.

Obviously, a big challenge today for any big IT department is coping with the sheer volume of information passing through and being processed and stored by the systems that it controls. To make matters worse, the courts have placed a higher value on the need to retain certain kinds of records than on IT's need to run a cost-effective operation. This was made clear in *Applied Telematics v. Sprint*,[4] as previously alluded to, where a company was penalized for destroying information relevant to the litigation by overwriting the backup tapes that contained the information.

At the same time, the courts and many regulators are taking a closer look at the way organizations manage digital information. Instant messaging has evolved into a serious enterprise tool. The regulators have taken notice of this evolution, and in the securities industry have made clear that instant messages need to be retained by firms like any other piece of business correspondence.[5]

Digital Information Is Changing

More and more of the information generated and received by organizations has serious legal and regulatory ramifications. This information, such as digital contracts, invoices, patient data in healthcare, and order flow information in securities, has different storage and management needs than much of the other information generated by organizations. This kind of information is often referred to as "fixed" content that must be stored in a way that preserves its original form and content to comply with records and evidentiary requirements.

In addition, fixed content may need to be:

- Stored for longer periods of time than information that is more transitory.
- Stored in a way that can withstand an attack on its credibility or trustworthiness.
- Accessed in a variety of ways by a variety of users.

Some analyst groups predict that storage of this kind of information will drive an increasing amount of overall IT storage budgets in the foreseeable future. A survey by AMR Research shows that companies intended to spend 7.4 percent more in 2008 than in 2007 on governance, risk management, and compliance (GRC). In 2008 corporate budgets for these items were forecast to be more than $32 billion.

The survey further indicated that GRC services numbers have been decreasing over the previous several years as companies have become more efficient in their compliance activities. However, as companies increasingly comprehend the importance of risk, they report that they want and need guidance on how to manage that risk. Thus, the majority of funding for GRC initiatives were for consulting services, as opposed to direct technological investments. Two-thirds of budgets (approximately $21.5 billion) were designated for people-related expenses (services plus head count) in 2008.[6]

DEALING WITH THIRD-PARTY PROVIDERS

With companies increasingly using third-party storage vendors such as application service providers (ASPs) and storage services providers (SSPs), the question arises: How does outsourcing record storage affect the organization's responsibility to preserve and produce information for a lawsuit, audit, or investigation?

Continues

DEALING WITH THIRD-PARTY PROVIDERS (*Continued*)

In most situations, just because records are not in your facility or in onsite computers does not mean that you are no longer responsible for preserving them or making them available. If a vendor is acting on your behalf according to a contract, you better make sure they are doing exactly what you would do if the records were stored on your premises—or you might end up paying for their mistakes.

How to protect your organization when a third-party is involved:

- Make sure that you, not the storage vendor, set retention rules for your records at their facility or in their computers. Your two organizations will have different exposure to liability in event of retention failure, so your motivation to properly retain information comes from different sources.
- Ensure that you have a mechanism in place to notify the vendor of an anticipated, filed, or ongoing investigation, audit, litigation, and/ or other formal proceedings that may require special preservation or production of information in their systems.
- Ensure that the vendor is contractually bound to cooperate with your requests for retrieval and production on your schedule, not theirs.
- Create clear contractual responsibilities delineating what happens if and when the relationship ends—your information is in their control and you are relying on their software and hardware.
- Ensure that adequate documentation of these activities is created and retained.

The fact that an organization's data is maintained by a third party does not affect the organization's responsibility to produce that data for a lawsuit, audit, or investigation. Federal Rule 34 requires the production of documents "which are in the possession, custody or control of the party upon whom the request is served." In *Tomlinson v. El Paso Corp.*,[7] a third-party human resources firm objected to the plaintiff's request for data definitions and field calculations of its proprietary human resources databases on the grounds that they were trade secrets. The court emphasized that the concept of "control" over the rule includes not only possession but also the "right, authority or ability to obtain the documents." Because the suit also involved an employee benefit plan, the defendant employer was subject to

DEALING WITH THIRD-PARTY PROVIDERS (*Continued*)

the Employee Retirement Income Security Act (ERISA). Under ERISA, the employer is obligated to ensure that its employee benefit records are "accessible...in such a manner as they may be readily inspected or examined." Thus, the court concluded that the defendant had (or should have), the "authority and ability to obtain the requested data."

One of the more exotic applications of this rule occurred in *Columbia Pictures Industries v. Bunnell*.[8] Columbia Pictures had sued the defendants for copyright infringement as a result of defendants' illegal distribution of Columbia's movies over the Internet. The court applied Rule 34 to require defendants to produce the IP addresses of users accessing the movies stored on the servers of third parties. Even though the IP addresses were stored in the random access memory (RAM) of the servers, the court directed that the defendants require the third parties to make electronic copies of the IP addresses of the log files containing the addresses.

The Impact of Sarbanes-Oxley on IT/IS Management

Although Sarbanes-Oxley is aimed directly at public companies, all organizations should pay attention to the focus that it puts on ensuring that internal controls within an organization are adequate to ensure that financial information is accurate and trustworthy. Simply put, organizations cannot be sure that financial information, or any information of value to the organization, is trustworthy without being sure that the IT systems that manage that information are also trustworthy.

In this sense, the importance of Sarbanes-Oxley to IT/IS management extends beyond the precise dictates of the law to the era that it has ushered in—an era where IT/IS is increasingly "regulated." This is an era in which IT must be managed with a view not only toward technical performance and efficiency but also toward the impact of an ever-increasing range of laws and regulations. Table 12-1 illustrates the shift in thinking that is required in those who manage IT as a result of this changing landscape.

Table 12-1: IT Questions—Yesterday and Today

Questions IT/IS Asked Yesterday	Questions IT/IS Should Ask Today
Is our data available to those who need it, when they need it?	Is our data trustworthy and reliable, and is it acceptable to our regulators and auditors?
How much time and money can we save if we reuse e-mail backup tapes every 30 days?	How big is the fine going to be when the court finds that we destroyed e-mail evidence during the course of an investigation?
How can we make sure that our financial systems are always available?	How can we make sure that the financial reports our CEO signs are accurate, so we can keep him or her out of trouble?
Are electronic records admissible in court?	Do our electronic records have enough integrity and trustworthiness to be persuasive in court?
How much business will we lose if a virus or worm cripples our systems and those systems are unavailable to customers and suppliers?	How much money will the court award our customers and suppliers in damages when a virus or worm from our system cripples their systems?
What controls and procedures are going to help us maximize our storage and system resources?	What controls and procedures are going to ensure that e-records are retained in a trustworthy manner, for the length of time required by law or business needs?
How can we provide our employees with efficient access to databases and other repositories of company information?	How can we provide regulators, auditors, and the courts with access to the e-records and e-evidence that they require in a timely fashion, in a format they require, without exposing or releasing unrelated information?
How can we design our web application to minimize calls to the help desk?	How can we design our web application to capture a complete record of all user interactions for regulatory purposes?

The Total Cost of Failure (TCF)

In the technology world, there are typically two formal reasons given for purchasing new software or hardware.

1. To save money (i.e., by cutting costs through automation)
2. To make money (i.e., by creating new capabilities and opportunities)

In reality, the reasons that organizations buy particular software and hardware are much more complex. Purchasers may be driven by company culture, trends, fear, a good relationship with the vendor, or reasons that aren't exactly clear to anyone.

Whatever the case, it is clear that the formal reasons given typically change according to economic conditions. During the boom years of the 1990s, technology purchases were all about "sustainable competitive advantage," "leveraging synergies," and "the new economy."

In the economic downturn and general slowdown in the technology industry experienced in the first few years of the new century, technology buyers have become much more conscious of the bottom line, as they have in past downturns. In times like these, buyers begin to demand that new technology pay for itself in a reasonable timeframe.

There are many methods—some simple, some complex—for calculating whether or not a technology purchase will pay for itself. At their most complex, these calculations treat technology like an economic investment whose value can be determined using the same methods as those used for financial market options. On the other hand, the calculations can be as simple as this:

> *If I buy this robot for $200,000, it will allow me to eliminate*
> *one human employee that now costs me $50,000 each per year.*
> *Therefore, the robot will start to save me money in the fifth year.*
> *And, I won't have to supply any coffee.*

Of course, very few technology purchases are that simple, as the cost of ongoing maintenance for the robot, electricity, training for robot technicians, the serviceable life of the robot, union negotiations, lowered employee morale, and numerous other "hard" and "soft" factors would need to be calculated in order to get an accurate economic picture of the robot purchase.

Two of the most common models for calculating the economic feasibility of technology are Return on Investment (ROI) and Total Cost of Ownership (TCO). In their simplest application, these models are based on determining and predicting all the economic benefits of implementing new technology, and subtracting all the real and potential costs of the new technology, to determine whether the technology is a good idea economically.

$$\frac{\text{Total economic benefit}}{\text{Time}} - \frac{\text{Total economic cost}}{\text{Time}} = \frac{\text{Positive/negative \$}}{\text{Time}}$$

Total Cost of Ownership, then, is one method of calculating the economic consequences of taking the action of buying, implementing, and maintaining new technology.

TCF—Turning the Model on Its Head

One of the most common complaints heard from people involved in Information Management is that it is difficult to economically justify the expenditures necessary to "do it right." There is a seemingly constant battle between those in the company that see the risks of IMC failure, and those who hold the purse strings. Business managers are not typically rewarded for spending money on projects for which there is no easily understood economic benefit.

Although the reluctance to spend money on Information Management has changed somewhat as a result of the current business climate with its near daily parade of news stories about corporate malfeasance, organizations need an easy and consistent way to understand the economics of Information Management Compliance.

This is where our concept of Total Cost of Failure (TCF) comes in. TCF turns TCO on its head.

TRUE OR FALSE

Which of the following do employees use to circumvent IT storage limitations, which ultimately impacts e-di--scovery costs?

Store business content in:

A. Thumb drives
B. PST files
C. Online information storage services
D. Home computers
E. All of the above

If you answered E, you would be correct. Making information management and discovery more challenging in recent years has been the reality that when faced with limitation in what employees can and cannot save, they find ways to work around the limitations. Usually those arbitrary storage limitations have huge and painful consequences in the context of discovery.

Whereas TCO is about calculating the economics of taking action, TCF is about calculating the economics of failing to take action, or of taking the wrong actions. In that regard, TCF is a key tool in the GRC approach. TCF incorporates compliance and risk-based factors into the decision-making process, where previously, such considerations might have been given short shrift.

As with calculating TCO, calculating TCF is not a science, and requires organizations to make educated guesses about possible cost sources in the future, the likelihood of particular cost sources occurring, the dollar amounts attached to various cost sources, and other factors.

Determining TCF Cost Sources

The costs associated with Information Management failure can come from many "hard" and "soft" sources. In order for a TCF estimate to be valuable, it must include consideration of the full range of possible costs.

By taking even a brief look at one aspect of Information Management—electronic discovery—it becomes clear the sources of cost that add up to TCF are varied and can add up very quickly (see Chapter 9 for more information on electronic discovery).

What is the potential Total Cost of Failure to have an adequate base of technology and policies to respond to the requests of the courts, regulators, auditors, and other parties for electronic records and other information?

- **Search and retrieval costs.** In the past, courts have required organizations to search through massive volumes of e-mail, at great cost, to find information responsive to litigation.
- **New software.** Organizations may be required to buy special software or even develop their own software that will allow their data to be searched, compiled, copied, and/or translated into a different format.
- **Penalties for destruction of evidence.** The courts take such destruction of evidence very seriously, and as you have seen throughout this book, criminal and civil litigation can result.
- **Employee time lost to participating in e-discovery efforts.** This "soft cost" can in fact be the source of greatest expense, as dozens of IT and other staff are tied up in the discovery effort.
- **Forensic experts** for data recovery and testimony.
- **Technology experts** for custom coding.
- **Computers**, servers, and networks taken offline, or made unavailable.[9]

> ### TCF SOURCES OF BOTH HARD AND SOFT COSTS
>
> - Inconvenience to business and personnel
> - Lost employee time
> - Impact to system functionality
> - Loss of customer confidence
> - Lost organizational reputation
> - Cost of losing a claim, dispute, lawsuit, or audit
> - Court-imposed sanctions and penalties
> - Lost business or business opportunity
> - Business failure
> - Regulator's penalties and increased scrutiny

Quantifying TCF Risk

Information Management failures come in all shapes and sizes, from the innocuous to the catastrophic, occurring infrequently or on a regular basis. Central to assessing TCF is being able to assess the risk associated with a particular IMC failure, such as failing to comply with a regulation or not being able to locate information required to serve a customer's needs.

Quantifying risk is an art and science unto itself, but basic models, such as the one described below, can be employed to develop a useful profile of potential IMC failures and support decision-making processes.

There are three key variables that organizations should assess when considering the TCF of particular IMC failures, as follows:

1. **Likelihood.** On scale of 1–10 (1 being very unlikely, 10 representing certainty of failure) what is likelihood of experiencing a particular IMC failure?
2. **Frequency.** On a scale of 1–10 (1 meaning the failure would only occur once, 10 meaning the event is certain to occur periodically) how often would your organization experience the IMC failure?
3. **Magnitude.** On a scale of 1–10 (1 being inconsequential damage, 10 meaning catastrophic damage) what would the magnitude of the failure be?

Organizations can employ this model to measure the risk related to a particular IMC failure, and use this measurement to establish an acceptable

threshold of risk for potential IMC failures. Although this threshold will naturally vary by organization, in general, a result of 18 or over on this scale should
be enough to cause most organizations to investigate ways that the risk can
be addressed and mitigated.

The Risk Model at Work: An Example

A fictional scenario that draws from real-world scenarios can be used to illustrate how the TCF risk model may be used to help organizations in the IMC
decision-making process.

In this scenario, a brokerage company wants to assess the potential risk of
failing to retain and manage e-mail communications in accordance with SEC
regulations. The firm has already calculated TCO for the hardware, software,
training, maintenance, and other costs of buying and implementing a Records
Management system that will enable them to comply with the regulations.
However, they are interested in establishing a useful quantification of the
risk associated with not purchasing the system. The TCF Risk model outlined
above can help the firm with this exercise.

1. Likelihood

Question: What is the likelihood that a regulator will unearth the non-
compliance and penalize the brokerage company for failing to properly
retain and manage the e-mail?

Analysis: In the current business climate and given past SEC and NASD
actions related to e-mail retention and management failures (see Chapter
7 for more information), the likelihood of uncovering the failure seems
relatively high.

Estimated Risk: 8

2. Frequency

Question: How often will the firm's failure to retain and properly manage
e-mail cause harm to the firm?

Analysis: Until corrected, the activity will be the source of regulatory
problems with the SEC, NASD, NYSE, and perhaps several state regulators. Additionally, their failure can be used against the firm in the context
of litigation unrelated to these regulators. For example, in the context of
litigation, the firm could be sanctioned for failing to retain records of
business activities in accordance with the law, or for allowing e-mail
evidence to be destroyed. The event is likely to harm the firm repeatedly

until it is corrected, and may even continue to harm the firm after corrective action is taken.

Estimated Risk: 9

3. Magnitude

Question: What is the extent of the damage, costs, and other harm likely to be if the firm is found to be failing to comply with the e-mail retention and management regulations?

Analysis: Given that several brokerage companies have already been fined millions for the same IMC failure, it seems reasonable to expect that the direct costs of penalties could well be in the millions of dollars. Additionally, the costs of correcting the problem in real costs (software, hardware, training, etc. costs will likely be higher because correcting the problem in a reactive mode may not allow for competitive bidding), inconveniencing employees, and disrupting business may be even higher. Bad press may even be more harmful as investors and boards lose confidence in leadership, negatively impacting stock values.

Estimated Risk: 9

Overall Analysis

With a measurement of 26 (8-Likelihood, 9-Frequency, 9-Magnitude) the risk associated with failing to comply with the e-mail retention and management regulations is very high and indicates that the firm would be prudent to take action to prevent this failure from occurring.

QUANTIFYING TCF IN THE REAL WORLD

1. In Illinois, a consumer's debit and credit card information is stolen from a retailer's system by a hacker. Under the Illinois Consumer Fraud and Deceptive Practices Act, the deceptive practice must inure to the defendant's benefit. The consumer is able to meet this requirement, and keep her lawsuit alive, by alleging that failure by the retailer to follow its own security procedures enabled the retailer to save money.

    Richardson v. DSW, Inc., 2006 U.S. Dist. LEXIS 1840 (N.D. Ill., Jan. 18, 2006).

QUANTIFYING TCF IN THE REAL WORLD (*Continued*)

2. Although the case was ultimately reversed on appeal on other grounds, a jury awarded a plaintiff $1.5 billion when the judge instructed the jury to consider the allegations of the complaint as true after finding that both employees of the defendant as well as its counsel deliberately hid discoverable information and lied about it to the court. The judge had also invited the jury to consider an award of punitive damages.

    Coleman (Parent) Holdings, Inc. v. Morgan Stanley & Co. Inc., 2005 Extra LEXIS 94 (Fla. Cir. Ct. Mar. 23, 2005).

3. A company deliberately destroys e-mails after being instructed by its counsel to preserve them. The court instructs the jury that it can infer that the content of the e-mails would have been damaging to the plaintiff. The jury awards the plaintiff more than $29 million.

    Zubulake v. UBS Warburg, 229 F.R.D. 422 (S.D.N.Y. 2004).

Another Example: Verizon and the Slammer Worm

With respect to its actions taken to prevent or minimize worm attacks, we find that Verizon did not take all reasonable and prudent steps available to it...Thus, Verizon should be held accountable for its failure.

Maine Public Utilities Commission Order, 2003 Me. PUC LEXIS 181, April 30, 2003

Verizon, a telecommunications company, had service agreements to provide network services to several other telcos such as AT&T and WorldCom (now called MCI). According to these agreements, Verizon would pay a penalty to its customers if the availability of its networks fell below 99.5%.

According to the Commission adjudicating the matter, in January 2003, an Internet worm known as the "Slammer Worm," which can damage and severely degrade online performance, hit Verizon's Internet servers. Verizon took its network services offline for about a day and a half in order to remove the worm and to test and apply a security patch from Microsoft that would protect against further attacks.

During this time, network services were unavailable to Verizon's customers, resulting in a level of service that fell below agreed-upon standards. AT&T and WorldCom therefore argued that they should receive a rebate as stipulated in the agreement. However, Verizon argued that the Slammer Worm was an "extraordinary event" and "unforeseen circumstance" that they had no control over, so there should be no rebate.

In its ruling the telecommunications commission found that the patch to protect against the Slammer Worm had been available for "at least six months before the attack actually occurred," and Microsoft had "issued 'Critical' security bulletins and associated software patches at both six- and three-month intervals prior to the event. Despite these warnings, Verizon apparently chose not to install the appropriate patch."

As such, the commission sided with Verizon's disgruntled customers and awarded the rebate at a cost to Verizon of:

1. $62,000 cash rebate.
2. Loss of customer goodwill.
3. Precedent set by the decision means that the company will need to reevaluate its procedures for securing and maintaining its systems, which could result in costs such as consultants, new technology, and more staff.

Lessons Learned

Industry experts have commented that the next round of "asbestos-type" class action litigation (i.e., massive settlements, worldwide, lasting for years, industry-changing) could come from liability caused by information security breaches. It's commonplace for a virus to seize control of employees' contacts list and transmit and self-propagate their own virus by making it look like the e-mail and attachment (that contains the virus) came from a known contact or colleague. The virus spreads like wildfire and impacts your customers' networks and computer without you even knowing about it. Thus, lessons learned include the following:

- Costs for failure can come from unexpected sources. With the law still evolving on many issues around cyber-liability, organizations should be careful to consider all the risks from security failures. In addition to this case, there are other cases where organizations have suffered because of their own, or a partner or customer's, failure to maintain and secure their systems.

- Make sure that policies and procedures for applying security patches satisfy not only the technical needs for testing and interoperability but also the legal need to protect against the liability that can come from security failures.
- Find out if there are points in your networks or systems that could be open to security failures that could create liability for your organization.
- Reevaluate agreements with Application service providers and other parties with whom you have service- and performance-based contracts. Do these contracts stipulate what will happen if the service becomes unavailable due to an Information Security breach?
- Investigate the Information Security policies and practices of your service providers, partners, customers, and any other parties to which you would be vulnerable in the case of a security breach.

Notes

[1] Matt Padowitz and Brian Tretick, "Compliance, Convergence and How IT Fits," CIO.com, January 8, 2008.

[2] The Economist Intelligence Unit, "Closing the IT-Business Gap," 2008.

[3] Radicati Group, "E-mail Archiving Market, 2007–2011." May, 2007, Masha Khmartseva and Sara Radicati, Ph.D.

[4] *Applied Telematics v. Sprint,* 1996 U.S. Dist. LEXIS 14053 (D. Pa.).

[5] According to regulations such as: Securities and Exchange Commission (SEC) Rule 17a-4, National Association of Securities Dealers (NASD) Conduct Rules 3010 and 3110, and New York Stock Exchange (NYSE) Rule 440.

[6] AMR Research, "Governance, Risk Management, and Compliance Report, 2008–2009".

[7] *Tomlinson v. El Paso Corp,* 245 F.R.D. 474 (D. Colo. 2007).

[8] *Columbia Pictures Industries v. Bunnell,* 2007 U.S. Dist. LEXIS 46364 (C.D. Cal. May 29, 2007).

[9] This lists of e-discovery costs comes from "Electronic Discovery: From Novelty to Target," Randolph Kahn, ESQ., and Barclay T. Blair. Readers interested in e-discovery issues should consult this paper, available at the Kahn Consulting website at http://www.kahnconsultinginc.com

Key #3:

Proper Delegation of Program Roles and Components

Responsibility for the Information Management programs must be delegated only to those individuals with appropriate training, qualifications, and authority.

Key Overview

The first two keys established the roles that clear, consistent rules and guidelines and strong, visible executive leadership play in IMC. Every employee in an organization shares responsibility for compliance, but specific roles and responsibilities also must be created, and appropriate authority delegated to oversee specific program components.

This section explores the importance of properly delegating responsibility for IMC, and provides guidelines to help organizations build an Information Management organizational structure that will promote business interests and protect legal needs.

This section also provides a model organizational structure that you can use to evaluate your organization's current approach.

13

Create an Organizational Structure to Support IMC

IMC relies upon an organizational structure to ensure that people with suitable skills, training, experience, and authority are put in charge of IMC in different areas, and at different levels, of the organization. This is not an easy task, and many organizations have struggled to build an Information Management infrastructure that reflects the ongoing transition to electronic business processes, new laws and regulations, and changing business practices in general.

Organizations must have a clearly mapped out and articulated organizational structure for their Information Management program. Remember that Information Management is a permanent part of your organization's activities, so your organization should have a permanent Information Management Governance structure.

In this chapter, we will look at several strategies for delegating authority for Information Management and creating a personnel structure designed to ensure compliance. This is critical because improper delegation not only increases the likelihood that Information Management mistakes will be made but also can create serious liability for the company. In the next chapter we will look at an actual example of an Information Management organizational structure that you can use to evaluate your current approach.

Specialization Is the Reality

Many issues in the Information Management world increasingly require the participation and advice of specialists. The organizational structure of many companies already reflects this specialization through the creation of executive-level offices such as the chief privacy officer and chief security officer, to name two.

The shifting landscape of privacy law means that developing and implementing a privacy policy increasingly requires the participation of a privacy lawyer or consultant. Decisions need to be made, for example, about which jurisdiction's laws affect your organization.

Even determining if a specific law affects your organization can be challenging. For example, many organizations have required a lawyer's advice to determine *if* they are an entity covered by the Health Insurance Portability and Accountability Act (HIPAA), a complex statute dealing with privacy and many other issues in the healthcare industry.

Your Information Management team needs to be broad enough to cover the full range of legal, business, operational, and compliance issues that must be addressed, and deep enough to ensure that each of these issues is addressed comprehensively.

LEGAL AND IT MUST COLLABORATE

Legal and technology professionals increasingly need to work together to meet their organization's Information Management needs.

This means coordinating efforts to find, preserve, and produce information required for investigations, audits, lawsuits, and other formal proceedings—as neither department is likely to be able to successfully do it alone. For example, a technology department on its own may not be able to determine whether a particular e-record is relevant to a legal action, whereas the legal department may not even know that the information (such as a server log file) exists.

Training and Certification Should Be Standardized

The process used to determine if employees have the right qualifications for the job should be standardized as much as possible, not only because it will increase the likelihood that staff will have the right skills but also because it will demonstrate a consistent approach to Information Management to the outside world.

In addition to formal programs offered by postsecondary institutions, a variety of organizations in the Information Management world provide certification and professional designation programs that require varying degrees of training and testing. Some of these include:

- **CA**: Certified Archivist, offered by the Academy of Certified Archivists
- **CRM**: Certified Records Manager, offered by the Institute of Certified Records Managers
- **MIT**: Master of Information Technology, offered by AIIM International

Organizations should also consider offering standardized on-the-job training programs for Information Management program staff that establishes a consistent standard throughout the organization.

The courts, for one, often take an interest in the training, qualifications, and responsibilities of employees who testify on behalf of the company. The training and qualifications of the claimant's witness were at issue in *In re Vinhnee*.[1] American Express was attempting to recover credit card balances from a bankrupt party. The success of its claim hinged on its ability to establish the authenticity of the records listing the balances, as they were generated from AmEx's computer system. In addition to the normal evidentiary requirements for business records, AmEx was required to provide "an additional authentication foundation regarding the computer and software utilized in order to assure the continuing accuracy of the records." At the trial, it was plain to the court that the witness testifying regarding the system knew little about it. The trial court then gave AmEx the opportunity to address the problem by providing additional information, and continued the trial.

After reviewing the additional material provided by AmEx, the trial court found that AmEx had not established the witness's qualifications for testifying, and further, did not provide testimony that established that AmEx "conduct[ed] its operations in reliance upon the accuracy of the computer in the retention and retrieval of the information in question."

On the qualifications issue, the court stated:

> *The qualifications of the declarant were particularly important because the assertions regarding reliability and accuracy of the American Express computers were fundamentally conclusory and in the nature of opinion. While a "qualified" witness or person...need not be an expert, there needs to be enough information presented to*

demonstrate that the person is sufficiently knowledgeable about the subject of the testimony....Here, the declarant merely asserted that he is employed by American Express and is personally familiar with the hardware and software and computer record-keeping systems in use in the credit card industry. He did not indicate his job title or anything about his training and experience that would import an aura of verisimilitude to his assertions.

The failures of AmEx in this regard were particularly noteworthy, as the court "added salt to the wound by noting that [AmEx] would have prevailed on one of two counts if the records had been admitted."

The lesson from our point of view is that Information Management in the electronic age calls for specialized expertise. In the paper world context, the witness might have been perfectly suited to attest to the authenticity of a customer's statement, but not in the electronic age. Similarly, the people responsible for Information Management in various areas of your organization must have different (probably more prodigious) skills, knowledge, and training than they did in years past.

"EXTRAORDINARILY POOR JUDGMENT" COSTS CEO

As explored in detail in Chapter 10, the case of *Danis v. USN Communications*[2] provides excellent insights into what the court considers good practice in the management and delegation of Information Management program roles and responsibilities. In this shareholder class action lawsuit, the judge found the CEO personally responsible for failing to take an active role in the company's record retention program, and fined him $10,000.

Specifically, the court stated that the CEO "was at fault for delegating" responsibility for preserving company records "to a person who lacked the experience to perform that job properly." The person in question was an in-house attorney with no litigation experience or experience in developing a retention program. The courts also said that the CEO "exhibited extraordinarily poor judgment" by delegating these responsibilities to the attorney, even though he had the option of using the company's outside law firm with deep experience in the area.

Competing Needs: Why Your
Committees Need to Be Broad and Deep ——

Consider this scenario: A manufacturing company deletes all e-mail messages older than 60 days, unless employees have moved them from their inbox to a shared or local hard drive.

However, the Sales Department announces that it wants to keep every e-mail message ever sent between the company and its customers. They even want to duplicate every message and keep one copy in the company's CRM system—forever—because they say the e-mail messages provide invaluable information about customers' buying habits and enable them to create more accurate sales forecasts. Customer Support agrees, and says that they can use the e-mail archive to create a "living library" of common customer complaints, frequently asked questions, and so on. They claim that customer support costs will drop as a result.

IT/IS isn't happy. They say the extra storage space will cost the company tens of thousands of dollars in extra hardware, maintenance, and staffing costs each year. Frankly, they think keeping e-mail for even 60 days is unnecessary and would like to see it "blown away" after 30. They also want someone to do something about staff clogging up shared network drives with their personal e-mail treasure troves.

Legal tends to agree with IT. The company's closest competitor has just come through a devastating lawsuit where damaging e-mails revealed that the company's engineers were aware of a potentially life-threatening flaw in the company's product. A multi-million dollar settlement ensued, their share price plummeted, and this competitor had to lay off employees. Although not unhappy about the competitor's fate, the head of Legal has been lying awake many nights since, wondering what horrors would be revealed in her company's own archives. She wouldn't mind if e-mail messages disappeared as soon as they were read, or better yet, that everyone just went back to using the telephone. For his part, the records manager thinks there must be a more disciplined approach to retaining e-mail that supports both business and legal needs.

Will Sales and Customer Support get their wish? Who should make that decision, and whose interests deserve top priority? Even though committees suffer from a reputation as being slow-moving, bureaucratic, and sleep-inducing, they may be the best answer here. Absent a highly placed, highly educated, multidisciplinary executive with too much time on his or her hands, it is unlikely that a single individual can, or even should, make the decision about what is best for the company in this type of situation. Each stakeholder in this example has a compelling argument.

The company clearly needs to find a solution that balances all departments' needs; one that promotes business needs while protecting legal interests. The only way this solution will be found is through a committee or council where the various stakeholders can communicate their needs and fears, and then work out a solution.

Perhaps the solution is in collecting only the essential information from customer e-mails and entering it into the CRM system to make Sales and Customer Service happy, then deleting the e-mails once they are no longer needed for legal or other purposes to make Legal and IT/IS happy. Perhaps there are technological solutions that can help the company retain e-mail based on content.

Whatever the case, the right solution depends on clear communications among all the stakeholders.

Who Should Be Responsible?

As technology, laws, and the business environment continue to evolve, there is undoubtedly confusion in many organizations about what department or individual should be responsible for specific aspects of IMC. Who should spearhead the effort? Is it better to have a senior executive or the resident subject matter expert (e.g., a lawyer, technology professional, Records Management specialist) communicate with the company about IMC policies and procedures?

A survey of large U.S. industrial companies completed by ARMA International found a great deal of variance amongst organizations in structuring Information and Records Management programs. For example, although most organizations in the survey placed Information and Records Management responsibility within one of two departments (business services or legal), the survey found 11 other departments were also used.[3]

Answer the following questions to illustrate some of the issues in this area that may seem subtle, but nonetheless can have an enormous effect on the success of your Information Management program.

1. A health insurer assembles a committee to deal with HIPAA. On the eve of disseminating the new company privacy policy via e-mail, the company

decides to place the name of the committee in the "From" field of the e-mail and at the top of the policy itself, to give credit to all who participated. Do you think having the committee's name on the e-mail, rather than the CIO's name, is the best way to get attention of all 40,000 employees?

2. The knowledge management director sends out a memo to the various business unit heads seeking their participation in a new databases sharing initiative, which would enable cross-selling to customers. Was she the right person to carry the banner for the new company project?

3. A records analyst contacts the information security director seeking help in gathering information requested in a subpoena from a regulator. He figures that the head of Information Security would be the right place to start. Is he right?

While the right answers to these questions depend on a number of factors, including the unique nature of each organization, the questions illustrate the challenges that organizations face when deciding who should be responsible for Information Management program elements.

While the committee members in the first question clearly understand the issues at hand, they may not be the best choice to carry the new policy banner forward. Important changes like this require the visibility that only high-level executive involvement can typically provide.

In the second question, the head of a department designed to serve the needs of the business units is not likely to have the authority or visibility to compel the business unit heads to expend time and energy on a project that does not have the blessing of corporate executives.

Finally, in the third question, although the information security director clearly may have a role to play in helping the company gather information responsive to the subpoena, there are complex legal issues at play that must be addressed and managed by the company's legal department.

DELEGATION MAY BE THERE, EVEN IF IT'S NOT ON PAPER

In *United States v. Van Riper*,[4] a gas station company was convicted of violating several regulations because of the acts of one of its managers. The company argued that only the manager, and not the company, should be held accountable for the violations. The company argued that the company "bore no responsibility" for the acts of the manager, as his illegal acts were not "within the scope of his authority."

Continues

DELEGATION MAY BE THERE, EVEN IF IT'S NOT ON PAPER (*Continued*)

However, the court found that the head of the company had "in effect delegated...full authority to conduct that gas station," to the manager, so his illegal acts were within the scope of his responsibilities. Thus, the company itself could be charged with the manager's violations.

The court went on to say:

If [a manager] caused the corporation to violate the law, then the corporation can be held liable even though the officers and directors of the corporation were ignorant of what actually was done...Otherwise a corporation could escape criminal liability by the simple expedient of the persons responsible for its corporate existence and management failing to perform the functions imposed upon them by corporation law.

In other words, organizations have a duty to supervise the activities of employees to whom they delegate authority, and to ensure that those employees can adequately do their job.

Notes

[1] *In re Vinhnee*, 336 B.R. 437 (B.A.P. 9th Cir. 2005).

[2] *Danis v. USN Communications, Inc.* 2000 WL 1694325, N.D.Ill., 2000.

[3] Saffady, William, and ARMA International, "Records and Information Management, A Benchmarking Study of Large U.S. Industrial Companies," 2002.

[4] *United States v. Van Riper*, 154 F.2d 492; 1946 U.S. App. LEXIS 2070.

14

A Sample Information Management Organizational Structure

Although the number of possible ways to create an Information Management organizational structure is probably the same as the number of different organizations doing business, there are some basic concepts that all organizations can use.

This chapter presents one possible model for an Information Management organizational structure. It is based on models used by many large institutions across the country. Its specific makeup and components will vary by organization, depending on size and other factors, but the basic elements and approach should help all organizations evaluate their approach to Information Management.

About This Model

This model Information Management organizational structure is designed for a large company with a central corporate entity and several business units that operate with varying degrees of independence from the corporate entity. Both the corporate office and the business units are further divided into departments. Smaller organizations also need to ensure that they have an organizational structure appropriate to ensure IMC, even though they may not have the human or financial resources to adopt a model with the scale of the one outlined here.

The model structure is designed to be implemented by a central corporate entity, which then "distributes" the structure to the various units in such a way that there is consistency across the entire organization, yet enough flexibility for "special cases" to be dealt with appropriately. For example, the various committees and councils across the entire organization use a consistent naming convention, which helps to clarify that their mandates are the same, no matter where they reside within the organization. On the flexibility side, however, individual business units have the ability to create special committees to address issues unique to their unit but not easily addressed by the "central" committees' staff or by the corporate Information Management department.

The model has two basic parts. First, it identifies the various committees and councils that compose the organizational structure, and explains their roles and responsibilities. This first part of the model is written in a formal manner, as you might find it in an Information Management manual or similar policy.

The model's second part describes the various individual roles that designated staff members play in the Information Management program.

The Councils

The Executive Information Management Council is at the top of the Information Management organizational structure. Executives from the various stakeholder departments throughout the corporation populate this council.

The stakeholder organizations in this example are:

- Legal
- Human Resources
- Information Technology/Information Systems
- Finance
- Records Management
- Business Risk Management
- Tax and Audit
- Compliance
- Affected business units

Although you may not have all of these departments in your organization, or they may have different names, this list illustrates the need to form a group that is large enough to encompass an appropriate range of business functions without being unwieldy.

The Information Management Committees

The Council has the ability to create multidisciplinary committees at the corporate level. Since corporate-level committees address high-level issues, they must be broadly based. High-level issues may include, for example:

- Privacy
- Sarbanes-Oxley

- Records retention
- Legal Hold and e-discovery
- Electronic records

This basic structure of a high-level council and subordinate committees (some of which will be addressed in this section) is duplicated at each business unit, with the only difference being that representatives come from the related business unit, and their primary focus is limited to Information Management issues within their unit only.

Individual Roles and Responsibilities

As explored in the previous chapter, organizations must assign specific Information Management responsibilities to qualified and experienced people, including the following:

- **Information management director**. A corporate executive with oversight of the organization-wide Information Management program.
- **Information management managers**. Business unit-level managers with responsibility for the Information Management program within their business unit.
- **Information management coordinators**. Department-level, "on-the-ground" experts with day-to-day responsibility for the Information Management program in their department.
- **Responsible attorney**. The corporate attorney responsible for issuing Legal Hold Orders.

The Model

The following model is for informational purposes only. Get the advice of counsel before adopting any such organizational model.

A. Executive Information Management Council

The Executive Information Management Council ("Council") shall have company-wide responsibility for ensuring that the Information Management

Program is implemented throughout the company. It shall also ensure that Information Management policies and procedures are in place to address operational, legal, and technical needs and requirements.

The Council shall meet periodically and shall be coordinated by the Information Management Department. The Council shall be composed of representatives from the Legal, Human Resources, Information Technology, Finance, Information Management, Business Risk Management, Tax and Audit, and Compliance departments. Specific activities of the Council and its Committees shall include, but not be limited to, assisting in the reviewing and approving of Policy, Retention Rules, storage practices, implementation of the various aspects of the Information Management Program, and development of new policies, rules, or directives regarding records, as needed.

The Executive Information Management Council shall create and oversee the Committees outlined below. The Council may create additional Committees as required.

Executive Records Retention Committee

The Executive Records Retention Committee ("Retention Committee") shall be responsible for drafting, reviewing, approving, and implementing the company-wide Retention Rules. The Retention Committee shall be composed of representatives from the Information Management, Legal, and Compliance departments, at a minimum. Specific activities shall include, but not be limited to, soliciting feedback and approval from the heads of affected Business Units when the Retention Rules are updated, and approving any records disposition.

Executive Records Preservation Committee

The Executive Records Preservation Committee ("Preservation Committee") shall be responsible for drafting, reviewing, approving, and implementing policies and procedures related to the preservation of electronic or paper records required for threatened or current audits, investigations, and/or litigation. The Preservation Committee shall be composed of representatives from the Information Management, Legal, Tax and Audit, and Information Technology departments, at a minimum. The Preservation Committee's activities shall include, but not be limited to, creating and implementing a process for the issuance, management, and termination of Legal Hold Orders.

Executive Electronic Records Committee

The Executive Electronic Records Committee ("E-Records Committee") shall be responsible for drafting, reviewing, approving, and implementing policies and procedures relating to the management of electronic records. The E-Records Committee shall be composed of representatives from the Information Management and Information Technology departments, at a minimum. Specific activities shall include, but not be limited to, addressing any electronic records issues and developing policies and procedures relating to electronic records.

B. Business Unit Information Management Council

Each Business Unit, under the direction of the Executive Information Management Council and the Information Management department, shall develop a Business Unit Information Management Council, which shall be responsible for activities similar to those undertaken by the Executive Information Management Council, with the functional difference being the limitation of scope to their specific Business Unit. Business Unit Information Management Councils and Committees shall be composed of Business Unit representatives from the same departments as those comprising the Executive Records Councils and Committees. In addition to addressing the issues of Records Retention, Legal Holds, and Electronic Records, each Business Unit Information Management Council and its Committees may also address additional or different Information Management-related issues impacting their Business Unit.

Each Business Unit Information Management Council shall create and oversee the Committees outlined below. Each Council may create additional Committees as required.

Business Unit Records Retention Committee

The Business Unit Records Retention Committee ("Retention Committee") shall be responsible for working with the Executive Records Retention Committee to ensure that the Retention Schedule (and other retention-related policies and procedures) meet the Business Unit's legal, operational, and technical requirements. The Retention Committee shall also be responsible for ensuring that the Retention Schedule is fully implemented and adhered to throughout the Business Unit. The Retention Committee shall also sign off on any records disposition within their Business Unit.

Business Unit Records Preservation Committee

The Business Unit Records Preservation Committee ("Preservation Committee") shall be responsible for assisting the Executive Records Preservation Committee with the implementation of the Legal Hold Policy and other Legal Hold-related procedures and notification mechanisms. The Preservation Committee shall help to ensure that their Business Unit meets its ongoing responsibilities for records preservation related to specific Legal Hold Orders (including Litigation and Tax Holds). The Preservation Committee may undertake training of employees on records preservation issues within their Business Unit.

Business Unit Electronic Records Committee

The Business Unit Electronic Records Committee ("E-Records Committee") shall be responsible for assisting the Executive Electronic Records Committee by reviewing and implementing any policies and procedures specifically required to address the proper management of electronic records within their Business Unit. The E-Records Committee may undertake additional or different Electronic Records issues within their Business Unit.

C. Individual Roles and Responsibilities

Information Management Director

The Information Management Director shall have high-level primary responsibility for architecting and implementing the Information Management Program. All policies, rules, and procedures affecting records shall involve the Information Management Director. The Information Management Director shall have primary responsibility for:

- Developing and implementing the Information Management Program.
- Implementing the retention schedule.
- Managing the offsite storage vendor relationship.
- Assisting with Councils and Committees at the Executive and Business Unit levels.
- Assisting with implementation of the Legal Hold process.
- Training and oversight of Business Unit Information Management Managers.

Business Unit Information Management Managers

Each Business Unit shall appoint one or more Information Management Managers with responsibility for one or more departments within their Business Unit. Information Management Manager responsibilities shall include, but not be limited to:

- Administration of the Information Management Program within the Business Unit.
- Conducting Business Unit records training.
- Monitoring Business Unit compliance with the Information Management Program.
- Managing the proper disposition of records.
- Managing the implementation of Legal Holds and the general preservation of required records.
- Serving on their Business Unit Information Management Council.
- Managing Business Unit preservation and retention of all types of records, regardless of format or media (i.e., electronic, film-based, and paper records).
- Training and oversight of Information Management Coordinators.

Information Management Coordinators

Each Business Unit shall appoint one or more Information Management Coordinators with responsibility for one or more departments within their Business Unit. Information Management Coordinator responsibilities shall include, but not be limited to:

- Assisting with the implementation of, and compliance with, the Information Management Program and any records-related policies and procedures affecting their respective department(s).
- Helping to ensure compliance with the Retention Schedule, and implementing changes to the Retention Schedule.
- Overseeing daily operations relating to inactive records.
- Assisting in moving inactive records to offsite storage.
- Communicating and coordinating with offsite storage vendors.
- Assisting departmental employees with records-related issues and questions.

- Assisting with the disposition of records.
- Assisting with the implementation of Legal Holds and general preservation of required records.

Responsible Attorney

The Responsible Attorney shall be responsible for the implementation of Records Hold Orders for threatened and/or current audits, investigations, and/or litigation requiring the preservation of records and other potential evidence in the company's possession, care, custody, or control. Other responsibilities shall include, but not be limited to:

- Disseminating the Legal Hold information to all relevant employees, Information Management Managers, Business Unit heads, and the Information Management Department.
- Determining what records and other materials are covered by a Legal Hold, and so advising employees in a manner that provides sufficient notice and understanding about what actions employees need to take to preserve and produce records.
- Working with Information Management Coordinators and Information Technology staff to ensure that electronic records covered by a Legal Hold are preserved.
- Periodically issuing reminder notices to all key players to comply with applicable Legal Hold Notices.
- Periodically reviewing Legal Holds in effect to ensure that preservation is still required.
- Issuing a Notice of Termination of a Legal Hold when the relevant audit, investigation, or litigation has concluded.

IT E-Discovery Liaison

The IT E-Discovery Liaison shall interface between the IT and the Legal department or outside counsel for the coordination of e-discovery issues. This individual has in-depth knowledge of the company's information systems, but has sufficient understanding of the legal environment that he or she can understand discovery requests, and can assist in formulating an effective response to those requests. Other responsibilities of the IT Liaison shall include, but are not limited to:

- Ensuring consistency in responses to requests for information when the firm received discovery requests in connection with multiple lawsuits.
- Acting as a single point of contact for electronic information requests.
- Coordinating implementation of Legal Hold notices with the IT department and key players involved in litigation.
- Assisting in the development and execution of the company's litigation response plan (the development of legal and technical strategies for the identification, collection, processing, review and production of data in response to a discovery request or preservation order).
- Acting as the firm's subject matter expert on IT systems for depositions (pursuant to Federal Rule 30(b)(6).
- Representing the IT department in early-stage "meet and confer" discovery conferences required under Federal Rule 26(f).
- Assisting counsel in responding to requests for information considered "not readily accessible" under Federal Rule 26(b)(2)(b) by documenting the technical and cost basis for "inaccessibility".

Key #4

Program Communication and Training

The organization must take steps to effectively communicate Information Management policies and procedures to all employees. These steps might include, for example, requiring all employees to participate in training programs, and the dissemination of information that explains in a practical and understandable manner what is expected of employees.

Key Overview

Once your organization's leadership supports and promotes your Information Management policies and procedures, the Information Management organizational structure is in place, and the right policies and procedures have been created, the organization must take steps to effectively communicate the policies and procedures to all employees.

15

Essential Elements of Information Management Communication and Training

Case after case has demonstrated that, whether they like or not, companies and government agencies can be held accountable for their failure to adequately train and monitor their employees' actions. IMC depends upon a comprehensive and consistent ongoing program of communication and training. Organizations cannot expect their managers and staff to comply with Information Management directives unless they are given the guidance and training they need.

The low degree of employee understanding of their IMC obligations reflected in the Kahn Consulting survey (see Chapter 4) reflects the fact that most organizations still have a lot of work to do in the training area, despite the fact that 67% of those surveyed stated that employee training is critical to their success.[1]

Be Clear and Consistent

Some time ago, a happy eBay bidder purchased a used BlackBerry, a mobile e-mail device that normally sells for hundreds of dollars new, for less than $20.[2] The seller was a former VP at a major investment bank who had left the firm months earlier and no longer needed the device.

When the buyer powered up the BlackBerry, he found that it contained a wealth of information, including:

- About 200 internal company e-mails that revealed information such as loan terms for various investment bank customers, nonpublic information about mergers and restructuring, and discussions with a customer about whether or not they should strictly adhere to the terms of contract.

- A database containing the contact information (in some cases, even home phone numbers) of more than 1,000 of the bank's employees, including senior executives.
- Personal e-mail messages revealing the VP's brokerage account numbers and mortgage payment amounts.

In this case, the company and the VP got very lucky, because the buyer was a "good guy" who reported his find. However, the potential implications of the information getting into the wrong hands are staggering, and can include:

- **Contract and privacy violations.** Violations of customer contracts, and privacy and confidentiality agreements
- **Espionage.** Loss of trade secrets and business intelligence to competitors
- **HR.** Loss of key executives to headhunters armed with personnel information
- **Regulatory.** Violations of securities laws concerning the release of non-public information affecting public companies
- **Internal policies.** Violation of internal data protection policies, employee privacy policies, and other policies and procedures

How Did This Happen?

The cause of this near disaster seems to have been a combination of a lack of training and inconsistent policy enforcement.

For his part, the VP allegedly thought that by removing the battery, all information on the device would be erased, although the device's memory does not require battery power to function. He also thought that when the bank (his former employer) terminated his e-mail account on the day he left the company, e-mail records residing on the device would also be deleted, which is not how the technology works. Rather, data can only be erased manually by using the device's syncing software, or remotely through a command from a properly configured server. The VP simply had not been trained regarding the compliance aspects of his device.

As for policy enforcement, the bank did have a policy that requires employees to return any mobile devices belonging to the firm before they leave the company. Simple enough, but in this case, the device did not belong to the firm—it was purchased by the VP using his own money and then configured to access the firm's e-mail system by the bank's IT department. It that case, the company says that their policy requires a departing employee to hand the device in for erasure before they leave—a policy that clearly was not enforced in this case.

There are any number of reasons why the policy was not enforced. Perhaps an HR employee was reluctant to demand that a senior executive hand over his BlackBerry. Perhaps the HR employee was not aware of the policy. Perhaps they both believed that removing batteries was enough.

Whatever the case, organizations need to ensure that sensitive information is adequately protected, regardless of where it resides. This is done through promoting awareness of the capabilities and Information Management implications of the technology employed throughout the organizations, ensuring that policies and procedures reflect those capabilities, and, finally, ensuring that these policies are enforced consistently, regardless of how awkward or sensitive that may be.

Clarity Is King

In Key #1, Chapter 7, we talked about the need to create policies and procedures that are clear and unambiguous. However, this careful work will be undone if communication and training related to the policy is unclear. This was clearly illustrated in *Garrity v. John Hancock Mut. Life Ins. Co.*,[3] where two female employees were terminated because they violated the company's e-mail policy that prohibited "messages that are defamatory, abusive, obscene, profane, sexually-oriented, threatening, or racially offensive."[4]

The policy also expressed very clearly that the company reserved the right to review and inspect e-mail sent or received on the corporate e-mail system.

Despite these policy elements, when a fellow employee complained about sexually explicit e-mail being sent and received over the corporate e-mail system, and the company reviewed the offending e-mail messages, the plaintiffs claimed that their privacy had been violated. Among other things, in their wrongful termination and defamation suit against Hancock, they asserted that the employer had violated their privacy because it "had led them to believe that these personal emails could be kept private with the use of personal passwords and email folders."

So despite the fact that the employer had written clear policies regarding e-mail privacy and the company's right to review employees' e-mail, it had also sent mixed messages to employees. Perhaps by allowing employees to create folders specifically for personal e-mails, protected by different passwords, they created the impression that—policy notwithstanding—those e-mail messages would be private.

Organizations need to be careful to be clear and consistent—not only in the language of policies and procedures but also in the way they communicate with employees about all Information Management issues.

Be Concise

Disseminate to your employees only those policies and procedures that they need to fulfill their Information Management obligations. You may also need to provide supplementary information that explains or supports the Information Management policies and procedures, and you may even want to give employees related but nonessential information that they might find useful or interesting, as long as it is concise and focused.

But do not overwhelm employees with extraneous or excessive information—that only sends a message that you do not value their time and haven't done your homework, and increases the likelihood that the information (even that which is on point) will be ignored altogether.

In our consulting practice, we have seen too many companies include information about firewalls and security administration, for example, in Records Management manuals. The procedures for properly configuring a company firewall, though undoubtedly full of amazing intrigue and plot twists, are completely useless to an administrative assistant, or a CEO for that matter. The same goes for intricate procedures dealing with offsite storage vendors in companies where only Records Management staff ever have dealings with those vendors, and so on.

Unnecessary information like this works against good Information Management program communication and training, not for it.

Be Visible

All executives, managers, and staff with designated responsibilities for Information Management program components must offer consistent and visible support for the program. In addition, the policy and procedure communications to employees must be consistent, regardless of where they are situated within the organization.

As explored earlier in the Leadership section (see Chapter 12), it is critical that top executives demonstrate their support for the Information Management program by communicating its importance directly to employees. This can be done through e-mail messages, voicemail blasts, face-to-face presentations, teleconferences, and many other ways as appropriate, depending on the size and culture of the organization. Regardless of the method used, it is important that the communications be consistent with the messages provided elsewhere by the program's policies and procedures.

This leadership message must then be carried forward by every level of the Information Management and Records Management team as they manage, coordinate, and implement the program.

It is also important that those responsible for day-to-day Information Management tasks be visible and approachable. Each employee needs to know who is responsible for answering questions, supervising, and assisting them with the Information Management task in their area, and know how to reach them. One way to ensure that this happens is by fostering an environment of "customer service" among technology personnel responsible for Information Management—for example, by measuring performance and compensating them on this aspect of their jobs.

Be Proactive and Responsive

It is critical that organizations be proactive in communicating Information Management program elements to all employees in a timely fashion. This means that organizations must:

- Address problems as soon as they arise
- Anticipate problems that may arise in the future and take steps to address them now

This is especially the case when employees have information in their possession that needs to be preserved because it is relevant to potential or current litigation.

For example, in *Testa v. Wal-Mart Stores*,[5] a truck driver successfully sued Wal-Mart for negligence because he slipped on an icy loading dock while making a delivery of tropical fish to a Wal-Mart store.

Wal-Mart appealed, claiming that the dock was icy because it was not accepting deliveries that day due to a grand opening celebration. The vendors, including Mr. Testa, were told not to make delivers. Therefore, Wal-Mart had not cleared the loading dock. Wal-Mart further claimed that, despite having been informed that Wal-Mart was not accepting deliveries on that day, Testa still made the delivery; and Wal-Mart warehouse staff felt obliged to receive the order of tropical fish.

However, in the case, Wal-Mart was unable to produce purchase orders or telephone records supporting its claim that it had warned Testa. An invoice clerk had disposed of these records before the trial began, "pursuant to a standard record-retention policy." The invoice clerk testified that "she did not know about the accident at the time and no one instructed her to preserve either the purchase order or the telephone records."

The court makes clear that it may assume that the contents of documents destroyed by a party, when they know that the documents may *potentially* be relevant to current or *potential* litigation, were in fact "unfavorable to that party." As the court clarifies, this idea

> *springs from the commonsense notion that a party who destroys*
> *a document (or permits it to be destroyed) when facing litigation,*
> *knowing the document's relevancy to issues in the case, may well do*
> *so out of a sense that the document's contents hurt his position.*

The court found that Wal-Mart had failed to inform the invoice clerk about the need to preserve records relevant to the accident. Wal-Mart had conducted an internal accident investigation immediately after the incident, and had also produced a report noting that it was likely that Testa would sue.

Moreover, the court states that the most relevant issue when determining what the consequences of improper document destruction (spoliation) should be is not the specific knowledge of the employee who destroyed the record:

> *[T]he critical part…depends, rather, on institutional notice—the*
> *aggregate knowledge possessed by a party and its agents, servants,*
> *and employees.*

In other words, since Wal-Mart knew about the accident and the likelihood of ensuing litigation, it had an obligation to inform all employees of the need to preserve information potentially relevant to that litigation. A jury is free to interpret a company's failure to provide this notification, and thereby allowing evidence to be destroyed, as an indication that the contents of the destroyed documents would have been damaging to the company's case.

This case illustrates the need for organizations to be proactive when dealing with all Information Management scenarios where they have a reasonable expectation that records may be needed in the event of a dispute or regulatory matter.

DUTY TO COMMUNICATE A LEGAL HOLD

A Legal Hold is useless if the company's employees, who generate the majority of the documents, don't know about it. Communication of a Legal Hold is an essential element, and courts have taken the failure to communicate a Legal Hold into account in levying sanctions for discovery failures. In *Doe v. Norwalk Community College*,[6] neither the registrar nor the head of Human Resources of the defendant college was aware of the Legal Hold. This contributed to the court's finding that the college's failure to institute a Legal Hold was grossly negligent, resulting in sanctions for the college. A failure to communicate a Legal Hold was implicit in the court's finding of bad faith in *Wiginton v. CB Richard Ellis*.[7] The defendant was on notice of its duty to preserve documents but failed to take any action to ensure that they would not be destroyed. "Its failure to change its normal document-retention policy, knowing that relevant documents would be destroyed if it did not act to preserve these documents, is evidence of bad faith." Timeliness of the communication was at issue in *Reino de Espana v. American Bureau of Shipping*.[8] The court held that issuance of Legal Hold notices more than a year after the incident (and six months after the suit was initiated) warranted a determination that the plaintiff had breached its duty to preserve evidence.

Offer Engaging and Interactive Training Programs

There is no excuse in today's technology-rich environment for offering static, dreary Information Management training programs that neither engage nor effectively educate the trainee. Aside from specialist computer programs designed for large companies with multiple training programs and thousands of employees, even the smallest company can inexpensively use a bit of Web programming and a small intranet to bring employees interactive and engaging training programs to help to bring the concepts of the Information Management program to life.

Intranet-Based

An organization's internal website, or intranet, can be a valuable resource in disseminating the information and training that employees need to comply with the Information Management program. An intranet can not only be used to provide directed training that includes video and other multimedia elements, but it can also provide a library of supplementary reference materials that employees may need as they are faced with various Information Management challenges.

For example, an intranet can be a great tool for providing information on Records or Legal Holds. This is not information that every employee needs every day, but when a group of employees are affected by potential or ongoing litigation, a prebuilt library of focused information about their specific responsibilities will be invaluable.

In addition, the intranet can be used to provide timely updates and notifications regarding Legal Holds and other urgent Information Management topics by providing links to the content in e-mail messages broadcast to the employees.

Instructor-Led Training

Even with advances in training technology that offer an array of interactive and entertaining elements for self-directed training, for many trainees there is no substitute for the human element. An experienced instructor can tailor his or her material "on the fly" to meet the needs of the group being trained, and can be much more responsive to questions and problems (as well as add humor and other engaging elements that are hard to duplicate in the self-directed environment).

Choosing to use instructor-led training over online or other forms of training can also send a message to employees about the relative importance of the topic. For example, bringing in outside instructors to talk about the importance of the Legal Hold process is likely to create a stronger impression on most employees than an e-mail message from their manager containing a URL for yet another round of Web-based training on the topic. Many organizations have used this approach in the past when their companies have been damaged by improper Information Management practices.

While face-to-face instructor-led training may not always be practical for large organizations with thousands of employees spread across the globe, many of the same benefits can still be offered by remote instructor-led training sessions that use video conferencing and interactive training materials.

Make IMC an Employee Priority

Although organizations may hope that each employee cares about the Information Management program simply because they are all highly ethical, motivated people who wish to act in the company's best interests, such thinking has unfortunately gotten too many organizations in trouble. While most employees in any given organization undoubtedly want to do the right thing, it is not that majority that causes the majority of the problems. In any case, it is not the ethical or responsible thing for the leaders of any organization to blindly hope that employees will educate themselves and comply with the Information Management program just because they are nice people.

Rather, employees need incentives to comply. In other words, give them a reason to care about the Information Management program by making clear to them that their compliance is an important aspect of their job, their compliance will be measured, and their compensation will be based in part on their compliance (the carrot). Also, make clear that a failure to comply will not be tolerated and may result in discipline, including termination and legal action (the stick).

Perhaps the most important—and most overlooked—aspect of encouraging employee compliance, however, is that *employees must be provided with the time and opportunity to fulfill their Information Management responsibilities and participate in the training programs*. Consider this example. A survey conducted by AIIM International and Kahn Consulting, Inc.[9] found that 65% of e-mail users spend at least a quarter of their working day writing, reading, and managing e-mail, and 25% of users spend more than half of their working day on those tasks.

Imagine a company where the majority of employees are spending a quarter of their time just coping with the daily e-mail flood. The company is just coming out of a lawsuit where several "smoking gun" e-mail messages were found in the e-mail archive that were very painful and damaging to the company—causing them to lose the case and a raft of customers too. So, the company has decided to change the way it manages e-mail. From now on employees will "manage it by content." The company has created a new Retention Schedule that identifies 75 different categories of records that they expect to find in e-mail and have provided this list of categories to the employees as part of a half-hour training session. At the session, the employees also learned that from now on they must manually select one of these 75 categories from a pop-up list in their e-mail program for *every e-mail message they send or receive.* The employees are told that this new "e-mail coding" process will help the company meet its legal obligations.

How much extra time do you think this new process will take each employee, each day? Another 5%, or 10% on top of the 25% of the day they already spend managing their e-mail?

Management has two choices. They can reduce employees' workload to provide more time to do their e-mail coding chores, and be realistic about how this change will affect employee productivity—and adjust their forecasts and expectations to match. Or they can make no realistic adjustment to their employees' workload, and have employees failing to complete projects on time, working longer hours, and generally suffering from lower morale. In the latter scenario, many employees will learn to cope in the way that is least likely to affect their performance: by hastily and improperly coding e-mail messages, thereby putting the company right back where it started with improperly managed e-mail records.

Too many organizations today are guilty of making the latter choice, and failing to give employees the tools (or time) they need to comply with critical Information Management policies and procedures. Without the tools, employees lose their motivation. Of course, the tools also need to be used and configured properly. In this case, the company should also investigate less time-consuming ways to properly code e-mail, by compressing the list of e-mail categories, and configuring the technology so that employees only see a customized list of categories that apply to their work.

Constantly Communicate and Train

Communicating with employees about the Information Management program is an ongoing process that should be a continuous part of an organization's culture and day-to-day operations. Although employees can learn Information Management fundamentals through one-time training sessions, ongoing reminders and refreshers will also be necessary. There are number of reasons why training must be continuous, as explored in the following sections.

Keep Current with the Latest Laws and Regulations

As explored in detail in Key 1, Chapter 7, an organization must keep its Information Management policies and procedures current with changes in the law and regulatory environment. This requires periodic review and updating of not only the core policies and procedures but also the communications and training materials used to support them.

Adjust to Major Events

Organizations also need to communicate with the employees when major events have a real or potential impact on the Information Management program. Events that should trigger communication from senior executives, managers, and/or Records Management staff include the following:

- **Mergers, acquisitions, and other major changes to the way the organization operates.** These upheavals often result in a change of culture, changes in the hierarchy of Information Management responsibility and authority, revisions of policies and procedures, new technology or reconfigurations of existing technology, turnover of committee membership, and so on.
- **New executives.** Changes in leadership may have a direct impact on who is responsible for Information Management and how the program is managed.
- **Changes in Information Management organizational structure.** Major changes to the Information Management organizational structure, such as the creation of new committees or roles, and the retirement of temporary committees or roles.
- **Terminations and other public disciplinary actions related to Information Management.** The mass firing of 40 employees for violating the company Internet use policy, theft of company information, or unauthorized use of unlicensed software undoubtedly requires authorization

from an organization's leaders. However, less spectacular, localized disciplinary actions, legal action, and termination can possibly be handled by department managers' HR representatives.

- **Litigation.** Lawsuits can precipitate an atmosphere of crisis, and senior executives must communicate with the organization to reassure employees and especially ensure that those who may have information in their care, custody, or control that is potentially relevant to litigation know exactly what to do.

Educate Employees about the Implication of New Technology

Changes in an organization's technology environment that affect employee's Information Management responsibilities should trigger new communication and perhaps training. For example, the adoption of desktop e-mail encryption technology would likely require updates to existing e-mail policies and training materials that explain to employees how to use the technology to encrypt the e-mail before they send it.

New technology can be exciting for employees, but it can also be a burden— just one more thing that they need to learn. So it behooves organizations to give the employees adequate training and support. Failure to do so could result not only in diminished productivity, but also serious liability, as illustrated by the BlackBerry device example provided at the beginning of this chapter.

New or updated technology may require employee communication and training on a host of issues, including:

- **How to use new applications securely.** Even the smallest mistakes can create big headaches for companies, such as employees opening e-mail attachments that contain viruses, or downloading "free" software from the Internet that contains keylogging "spyware." Employees need to be trained on the security do's and don'ts of new technology before it is deployed.
- **Appropriate uses of new technology.** Just because a piece of software or hardware can accomplish a particular task doesn't mean that it should be used in that way. For example, an employer-supplied PDA may be

able to send and receive an employee's personal e-mail, but that does not mean that the company should allow it to be used in that way. The intermingling of work and personal e-mail may create a range of privacy and professional issues that the company should avoid by providing a new acceptable-use policy that prohibits the practice—especially if the IT/IS department cannot prevent it through configuration controls.

- **Employee responsibilities.** Employees must clearly understand exactly what their responsibilities are in regards to new technology. For example, are they responsible for capturing their instant messaging conversations with customers and storing them somewhere, or does the software do it automatically?

- **Managing output.** Each new technology will likely generate information that must be managed. It is the company's responsibility to have rules in place before the technology is implemented, to ensure from the very beginning that information is properly managed. For example, BlackBerrys have both text messaging and e-mail capability. The e-mails can be synched with a central server and thus preserved, but text messages are not. The company may want to either implement a capability to retain text messages, but if not, must have a policy in place which prohibits business communications via text messages.

Notes

[1] "GRC, E-Discovery, and RIM: State of the Industry—A Kahn Consulting, Inc. Survey in association with ARMA International, BNA Digital Discovery and E-Evidence, *Business Trends Quarterly*, and the Society of Corporate Compliance & Ethics," (Fall 2008), p. 7, found at www. kahnconsultinginc.com/library/surveys.html.

[2] Zetter, Kim, "BlackBerry Reveals Bank's Secrets," Wired News, August 25, 2003. Online at http://www.wired.com/news/business/0,1367,60052-3,00.html

[3] *Garrity v. John Hancock Mut. Life Ins. Co.*, 146 Lab. Cas. (CCH) P59, 541.

[4] Ibid.

[5] *Testa v. Wal-Mart Stores*, 144 F.3d 173.

[6] *Doe v. Norwalk Community College*, 248 F.R.D. 372 (D. Conn. 2007).

[7] *Wiginton v. CB Richard Ellis*, 2003 U.S. Dist. LEXIS 19128 (N.D. Ill. Oct. 24, 2003).

[8] *Reino de Espana v. American Bureau of Shipping*, 2007 U.S. Dist. LEXIS 41498 (S.D.N.Y. Jun. 6, 2007).

[9] Email Policies and Practices: An Industry Study Conducted by AIIM International and Kahn Consulting, Inc., 2003.

Key #5

Auditing and Monitoring to Measure Program Compliance

The organization must take reasonable steps to measure compliance with Information Management policies and procedures by utilizing monitoring and auditing programs.

Key Overview

The best Information Management policies and practices in the world will not protect an organization unless they have the means to find out if employees are in fact complying with those directives. This is the role of auditing and monitoring—to provide management with a method of measuring and improving IMC. Auditing and monitoring are key components of a GRC program as well; companies cannot assess the effectiveness of their actions without a feedback mechanism.

16

Use Auditing and Monitoring to Measure IMC

An organization's work is not complete, even after it has drafted policies and has trained employees. Rather, organizations need to continue their commitment to IMC by establishing programs to audit and monitor compliance with the Information Management program.

Information Management Auditing and Monitoring

Auditing in the financial world is, of course, a formal discipline practiced by highly trained auditing specialists. The term *audit* as used in this book has a more general meaning that includes any practice designed to *periodically measure and report on compliance with a set of standards or criteria*. In this sense, auditing activities in the Information Management world are often referred to in many other ways, such as assessment, evaluation, review, survey, validation, and so on. Although these terms all have specific, formal meanings in a variety of financial, technical, regulatory, and operational environments, the focus of this section is not on differentiating among these activities but on exploring how their concepts can be used to help organizations increase IMC.

Monitoring is a related, but separate, concept. The goal of monitoring is generally the same as auditing, except that it is performed on an *ongoing* basis. So, Information Management monitoring is the *ongoing measurement and reporting on compliance with a set of standards or criteria*. In other words, Information Management auditing and monitoring are both designed to find out exactly what is happening in an organization, but auditing accomplishes this by looking at the past, whereas monitoring accomplishes this by looking at what is happening right now.

Together, Information Management auditing and monitoring provide a two-pronged management control that is essential for ensuring that an organization is meeting its Information Management goals and obligations.

Find Out before Someone Else Does

Putting it simply, Information Management auditing and monitoring matter because, as the saying goes, "If you can't measure it, you can't manage it." Auditing and monitoring allow organizations to understand where their Information Management program is succeeding and where it is failing, and correct any compliance problems before they blossom into full-fledged disasters. In other words, auditing and monitoring allow you to find out about your problems before someone else—like a court, regulator, auditor, or shareholder.

A few years ago our consulting firm was engaged to perform an audit of a large client's imaging system that used two parallel, identical, high-volume document scanners. During the audit we found that, although the scanners were identical, one had incorrectly been set up to scan documents at nearly half the resolution of the other. This configuration variance had not been discovered by the organization. Even though the client was confident that documents scanned at the lower resolution still adequately captured the information contained in the original paper documents, they had not considered the potential consequences of their configuration inconsistency.

We asked our clients to imagine themselves on the witness stand at trial, being cross-examined about the accuracy of the scanned electronic documents created by their system. We suggested that the exchange might look something like this:

> **Attorney:** So, because one scanner was set at nearly double the resolution, then did it technically capture more information?
>
> **Client witness:** Yes, well, I suppose...
>
> **Attorney:** So, is it possible that if a document that had lightly handwritten notes and comments on it, those notes would be picked up by one scanner and not the other?
>
> **Client witness:** Well, I suppose it is possible, but not likely.

Attorney: So, you are saying that it is in fact possible that an electronic document imaged by the low-resolution scanner may not actually contain all the information of the original document?

Client witness: Well, I guess…

Attorney: Are you aware that a central issue in this case is whether or not your company's electronic records are accurate, and whether or not this court can rely on them?

Client witness: Yes, I was told that, but…

Attorney: And yet, you sit here today and have told us that your system for scanning and imaging electronic records might be inadequate. And that it is possible that all the information found on an original paper records may not actually be captured by the low-resolution scanner, that…(and so on)

What is happening in this exchange is that the attorney is trying to raise doubt in the jury's mind about the company's scanning procedures. The company's own practices and their investment in high-resolution scanners indicated that they thought it was necessary to scan documents at the higher resolution. If the company itself believed that this was necessary, and yet did not do it consistently, how can they expect the jury to not have questions about the accuracy of the scanned records?

Had the company implemented an auditing or monitoring program that used techniques such as routinely comparing the file size or resolution of scanned documents, and so on, this the potential litigation issue would not have existed. What seems insignificant today might provide a litigator with ammunition tomorrow.

Auditing and Monitoring Programs Help to Build Trust

Developing and implementing good Information Management policies and procedures demonstrates to employees and to the outside world that the organization takes its Information Management obligations seriously. Developing and carrying out auditing and monitoring programs is the next step in demonstrating this commitment and building trust. These programs demonstrate that not only is the organization willing to spend the time and money required to develop the policies, but also to ensure that employees stay in compliance. Weighting such programs on a risk-adjusted basis (in accordance with a GRC philosophy), however, more efficiently allocates resources to those areas that require the most focus (i.e., most risky), while enabling cost savings in areas where the company has little exposure.

Besides, if you are reluctant to take your Information Management obligations seriously, the courts and regulators might force you to do so.

In *Qualcomm, Inc. v. Broadcom Corp.*,[1] the nondisclosures and misrepresentations of the plaintiff led the judge to conclude that it had engaged in "an organized program of litigation misconduct and concealment throughout discovery, trial, and post-trial before new counsel took over." Qualcomm's new attorneys subsequently found hundreds of thousands of pages of documents that had been requested but not produced in discovery. These documents "revealed facts that appear to be inconsistent with certain arguments…made on Qualcomm's behalf at trial and at the equitable hearing following trial." This misconduct resulted in sanctions against individual attorneys and the award of all of Broadcom's attorney's fees, which exceeded $8.5 million. In addition, the court ordered:

> *Qualcomm and the Sanctioned Attorneys to participate in a comprehensive Case Review and Enforcement of Discovery Obligations… program. This is a collaborative process to identify the failures in the case management and discovery protocol utilized by Qualcomm and its in-house and retained attorneys in this case, to craft alternatives that will prevent such failures in the future, to evaluate and test the alternatives, and ultimately, to create a case management protocol which will serve as a model for the future.*

The Securities and Exchange Commission went one step further during its investigation of WorldCom, imposing an $800-an-hour monitor on the company to ensure that the company did not destroy evidence of its accounting debacle, and that it had "developed document retention policies and… [had] complied with these policies."[2] The monitor was a former chairman of the SEC.

In these two cases, the companies were acting in a manner that apparently created suspicion with the court and the regulator, not trust. Their failure to carry out adequate auditing and monitoring placed them under increased scrutiny.

APPLICATION OF RETENTION RULES TO E-RECORDS

If there is any area that could use auditing in today's organizations, it is the proper retention and disposition of electronic records. Auditing in this area can include a range of activities, from complex system inventories, to a review of basic Records Management software configuration and functionality. At a minimum, organizations need to make sure that records are being retained for the proper length of time, whether the records are in paper or electronic form.

This was clearly demonstrated in a complex case in 2000 that dealt with excessive force allegations against the city of Columbus, Ohio police force.[3] A local newspaper requested police records, including complaints against city police officers. The city was required to retain disciplinary records under the state's public records laws, and their retention rules stipulated that the records in question be retained for three years.

Although the paper records had been destroyed in accordance with the retention rules, the city had not destroyed the electronic versions of these records. As a result, disciplinary records dating back almost 10 years were available in electronic form.[4]

A lengthy legal battle ensued over the release of the older records, with the court ultimately deciding that the city's failure to dispose of the records according to their own retention rules did not change the fact that the older records were still records that the public had the right to access. As such, the records were released to the newspaper.

Organizations need to ensure that paper and electronic records are being managed consistently, and that retention rules are followed regardless of where records reside or the medium upon which they are stored.

Know What Is Happening on Your Own Networks

A software company sued a competitor for electronic espionage. The company claimed to have found evidence in the log files of its private File Transfer

Protocol (FTP) server that showed that the competitor had been accessing the server over the period of a year. Over the course of the year, the company claimed, more than 900 sensitive files had been accessed and downloaded, including contact information for nearly 110,000 of the company's customers and prospects. The company also claimed that the competitor had downloaded confidential advertising materials and used them to create a nearly identical campaign of its own. According to the company, the competitor was able to gain access to the server by using the confidential username and password of an employee (and also an "anonymous" account), who was not suspected of being involved in the espionage.[5] If the allegations of intellectual property theft and espionage in this case are true, the company clearly had good reason to bring legal action.

Many organizations have found themselves in similar situations where they have suffered losses as a result of security breaches. This case, and others like it, illustrate the need for all organizations to be prepared to ask hard questions about their ability to monitor and audit activities on their own servers. In this case, questions such as the following should be asked:

- How did the outsider get access to the usernames and passwords of its employees? Was the outsider able to guess the passwords based on the employees' names or other data points? Were the passwords "bad" in that they were easily guessable or default system passwords? Does the company have a password policy and was it enforced?
- Why were the company's customer list and other "crown jewels" protected only by a username and password? To state the obvious, perhaps an FTP server directly accessible over the Internet is not the best place to house such valuable information.
- Why did it take the company over a year to notice the theft? If use was limited to internal staff only, then why was the company not monitoring the server for access from unfamiliar Internet Protocol (IP) addresses, or using related security techniques?

These questions are particularly relevant, given that FTP security vulnerabilities are well known. For example, the CERT Coordination Center (a noncommercial institution that tracks and advises on information security incidents) issued a public advisory in response to "a continuous stream of reports from sites that are experiencing unwanted activities within" their FTP areas. The advisory identified "improper configurations leading to system compromise" as one of the leading causes of the security breaches. The advisory also provided instructions on how to configure FTP to combat certain vulnerabilities.[6]

Auditing or Monitoring May Be Required by Law

Several laws and regulations require Information Management auditing and monitoring programs. Internal Revenue Service Revenue Procedure 97-22 is an excellent example of such a regulation.

Internal and External Audits: IRS Revenue Procedure 97-22

This IRS regulation provides requirements for taxpayers who wish to keep required records in electronic form, and describes several criteria that an electronic recordkeeping system must meet. Moreover, the regulation explicitly requires Information Management-style controls and audits.

For example, the regulation makes clear that an electronic storage system for records must include:

- **Security and other management controls.** "[R]easonable controls to ensure the integrity, accuracy, and reliability of the electronic storage system."
- **Monitoring programs.** "[R]easonable controls to prevent and detect the unauthorized creation of, addition to, alteration of, deletion of, or deterioration of electronically stored books and records."
- **Auditing programs.** "[A]n inspection and quality assurance program evidenced by regular evaluations of the electronic storage system including periodic checks of electronically stored books and records."[7]

The regulation also makes clear that the IRS has the right to periodically conduct its own audit of the taxpayer's recordkeeping system to ensure that it complies. This audit can be quite extensive and may include:

- **System evaluation.** "[A]n evaluation (by actual use) of a taxpayer's equipment and software."

- **Evaluation of procedures**. "[P]rocedures used by a taxpayer to prepare, record, transfer, index, store, preserve, retrieve, and reproduce electronically stored documents."
- **Additional review** of "internal controls, security procedures, and documentation."[8]

In addition, the IRS expects that organizations will also conduct their own Information Management audits. The regulation states that organizations that have converted original hard copy records to electronic form for storage may destroy the hard copy records *only* after they have completed an internal audit and established an ongoing auditing program.

> *This revenue procedure permits the destruction of the original hard-copy books and records and the deletion of the original computerized records...after the taxpayer:*
>
> *(1) has completed its own testing of the electronic storage system that establishes that hardcopy or computerized books and records are being reproduced in compliance with all the provisions of this revenue procedures, and*
>
> *(2) has instituted procedures that ensure its continued compliance with all the provisions of this revenue procedure.*[9]

Organizations can learn from the model used by the IRS in reviewing electronic record storage systems. It focuses on key areas of internal controls, policies and procedures, and actual system functionality—areas that are critical for any form of Information Management auditing or monitoring program.

Monitoring Programs: Supervision Under NASD Conduct Rule 3010

The Financial Industry Regulatory Authority, Inc. (FINRA), in conjunction with the Securities and Exchange Commission and other bodies, regulates the securities industry. The financial services industry in general, and the securities industry specifically, are viewed as among the most regulated industries, so their approach to regulatory compliance is closely watched by other industries.

A key FINRA Rule for securities brokers and dealers is NASD Rule 3010, which outlines a primary philosophy of the FINRA regulations—that its members have an obligation to actively supervise the activities of their employees on an *ongoing basis*.

FINRA requires that securities firms "establish and maintain a system to supervise the activities [of employees] that is reasonably designed to achieve compliance with applicable securities laws and regulations." In other words, an auditing and monitoring program. This rule, as it has been interpreted, applies to the supervision of employee e-mail correspondence.

Key elements of FINRA's mandated supervisory system include:

- Written procedures, including records showing to whom supervisory responsibilities were delegated in the organization. Companies are also required to keep their procedures up to date with "applicable securities laws and regulations."
- An "Internal Inspection," at least annually, which is "reasonably designed to assist in detecting and preventing violations of and achieving compliance with applicable securities laws and regulations," in other words, an internal audit.
- The creation of an office with specific responsibility for overseeing the supervisory program.

Monitoring Legal Holds

The courts have held that once a lawsuit begins, it is not enough to merely institute a Legal Hold. There is also an obligation to monitor compliance with the Legal Hold.[10] In *Zubulake v. UBS Warburg*,[11] the court explained the duty as follows:

> *To do this, counsel must become fully familiar with her client's document retention policies, as well as the client's data retention architecture. This will invariably involve speaking with information technology personnel, who can explain system-wide backup procedures and the actual (as opposed to theoretical) implementation of the firm's recycling policy. It will also involve communicating with the "key players" in the litigation, in order to understand how they stored information.*

As the *Zubulake* case indicates, the courts usually impose the duty upon legal counsel. However, it is not counsel that usually suffers the consequences. It is the client that must pay the sanctions that are levied as a result of the failure to comply, and it is the client who must pay the judgment if the jury comes back with a large verdict (a $29 million verdict in the *Zubulake* case) as a result of discovery violations.

Internal versus External Auditing and Monitoring Programs

While organizations need to adopt ongoing internal programs for auditing and monitoring their IMC, they also need to consider the role that independent third parties play in auditing and monitoring.

In some cases, organizations should consider the use of independent third parties to conduct period reviews and assessments of their Information Management program. This is particularly the case in highly regulated industries. For example, independent audits and assessments are common in the pharmaceutical industry (using 21 CFR Part 11, for example), the healthcare industry (using HIPAA), and the securities industry (using SEC 17a-4).

Such audits can be very formal and involve multiple steps, including a complete review of Information Management documentation, employee interviews, examination of "live" processes and technology in action, and so on. On the other hand, such audits can also be less formal, and limited to an offsite review of specific policies and procedures, for example.

The type of audit that is appropriate depends on many factors, including the stage that the target organization is in with their Information Management program, the size and number of locations and business units, the complexity of their technology environment, the legal and regulatory environment in which they operate, and the appropriate risk factors associated with the various systems operated by the target organization. For example, an organization that has just completed a revision of its Records Management manual, updated its retention schedule, and introduced a new e-mail archiving system is an organization that could likely benefit a great deal from an independent assessment of their Information Management program.

There are many models used for independent auditing and assessment, and their sources and methodologies vary by industry, audience, and intended result. For example, the American Bar Association has developed the *PKI Assessment Guidelines*, which provides a model for assessing the trustworthiness of an information security system.[12] This document provides a multidisciplinary assessment model that borrows from auditing and risk assessment models used in a variety of contexts, from the insurance industry to computer hardware testing and certification. Effective audits of Information Management programs at most large organizations similarly require a multidisciplinary approach that incorporates specialized legal, technological, Records Management, risk management, and other best-practices expertise.

Required Third-Party Involvement

In some cases, an organization may be legally required to seek out the validation of a third party. For example, SEC Rule 17 CFR § 240.17a-4 ("17a-4") requires a broker-dealer firm that wishes to store electronic records on certain types of media to "provide its own representation or one from the storage medium vendor or other third party with appropriate expertise that the selected storage media meets the conditions" of the regulation. Whether the firm prepares its own representation or has the vendor prepare it, the firm may be placed in a position of relying on a third party's validation and auditing procedures.

Also, IRS Revenue Procedure 97-22, explored in detail earlier in this chapter, specifically states that taxpayers who use a third-party service for storing their records are not relieved of their responsibility to ensure that the requirements of the Revenue Procedure are met. This means that the service provider should expect customers to request contractual assurances that their systems and procedures comply with IRS requirements, which in turn will require the service provider to conduct an internal audit, at a minimum.

Making Representations to Third Parties

On some occasions your organization may be required to make representations about your Information Management program to regulators, courts, auditors, and other third parties. The accuracy of your representations depends in large part on your ability to audit and monitor compliance with your own Information Management policies and procedures. In addition, the third party may require specific auditing and monitoring activities to ensure that your organization complies with its requirements.

As noted earlier, Sarbanes-Oxley requires public companies to make representations in their annual reports about their "internal control structure and procedures for financial reporting." These companies have to implement and operate extensive auditing and monitoring procedures to ensure that those representations are accurate and will not be a source of future liability.

Another instance where Information Management auditing and monitoring is essential for making representations to a third party is the U.S. Department of Commerce Safe Harbor program for privacy protection.

The European Union (EU) passed the European Commission's Directive on Data Protection, (the "Directive"), which among other things does not allow the transfer of personal information from European Union nations to any nation that does not meet the Directive's "standard of adequacy" for privacy protection. The Directive would have made some operations difficult for U.S. companies operating in EU countries, as it would prohibit them from transferring personal information regarding their European customers, for example, to their facilities in the United States.

The U.S. Department of Commerce, in consultation with the European Commission, developed the Safe Harbor program to address this situation. Safe Harbor effectively allows U.S. companies to comply with the Directive by adjusting their privacy practices to conform to the principles of the Directive. Companies that want to participate must complete an annual "self-certification" that represents to the Department of Commerce (and the public) that their privacy practices conform to the Safe Harbor framework.

The Safe Harbor contains seven "Privacy Principles" that companies must adhere to.[13] One of these principles, entitled "Enforcement," clarifies the need for auditing and monitoring programs to achieve compliance:

> *Effective privacy protection must include mechanisms for assuring compliance with the Principles…and consequences for the organization when the Principles are not followed. At a minimum, such mechanisms must include…follow up procedures for verifying that the attestations and assertions businesses make about their privacy practices are true and that privacy practices have been implemented as presented.[14]*

The Department of Commerce (DOC) also provides companies with guidance on the "mechanisms for compliance" that they should use, which include

Information Management auditing and monitoring programs. DOC states that companies can use "self-assessment or outside compliance reviews" that include such techniques as "random reviews, use of 'decoys,' or use of technology tools as appropriate."[15]

AUDITING AND MONITORING ARE REQUIRED TO PROTECT THE ORGANIZATION

There are many instances where organizations have an obligation to audit and monitor what is happening within its walls, both physically and virtually.

For example, the law requires that employers "take affirmative steps to maintain a workplace free of harassment and to investigate and take prompt and effective remedial action when potentially harassing conduct was discovered."[16] Without an effective program to audit and monitor the actions of its employees, it is difficult for an employer to meet this requirement.

As the court in *Garrity v. John Hancock Mut. Life Ins. Co.,*[17] states, "E-mail transmission of sexually explicit and offensive material such as jokes, pictures, and videos, exposes the employer to sexual harassment and sex discrimination lawsuits. Therefore, once an employer receives a complaint about sexually explicit e-mails, it is required by law to commence an investigation."

Piracy: Don't Look the Other Way

According to the Business Software Alliance, for every two dollars' worth of software purchased legitimately, one dollar's worth was obtained illegally, resulting in an annual loss of $48 billion to the software industry in 2007.[18] Although many companies have turned a blind eye to—or even implicitly endorsed—the common practice of installing a single licensed copy of a software program on multiple computers, in recent years software companies and lawmakers have become more aggressive about preventing this type of piracy.

It may be time to conduct a licensing audit, especially if Information Management assessments and audits are planned. For example, an inventory of the various types of electronic records created throughout an organization will also reveal much information about the software applications in use. This information can in turn be cross-referenced against vendor licensing agreements.

However, as with many issues, legal liability may be greater for organizations that fail to take steps to stamp out internal piracy once they know it exists. This means that you must be prepared to take action through policy, education, discipline, and other measures to deal with any piracy you may find.

Preventing piracy begins with creating the right culture. Your organization needs to send clear messages that piracy is not okay, and educate managers to promote this attitude.

Action Items

- Make sure that you have clear statements from senior management forbidding piracy. These are often appropriate coming from the CIO's office, particularly when issued in advance of a licensing audit, and should be included in employee policies and educational materials.
- Especially in small to medium-sized companies with limited IT budgets and centralized IT controls, watch out for employees installing pirated software on their own.
- Work to prevent your company from becoming a source for external piracy. Software applications purchased under a site license may have "copy protections" removed, which makes them easy to copy and disseminate. Closely monitor the use of such installation disks, and store them in a secure location.
- Applications provided by business partners can also be pirated, as copy protections are often disabled or reduced, and employees may feel the business relationship entitles them to use the application for free. However, unless such use is explicitly covered by partnership agreements, do not assume that it is permitted.

Monitoring Employee Activity

Information that can be found and logged on employee computers includes:

- A record of every software application that was run
- Both sides of instant messaging and chat conversations
- Text and images that were copied to the clipboard
- Keystroke monitoring—a record of every key pressed on a keyboard, and the window in which they were pressed

- A log of processor and memory load, processes running at any given time, and the temperature of the computer's CPU
- Every website visited and the pages that were viewed or other information that was downloaded
- The names of all documents printed
- Internal network locations visited
- Presence monitoring, that is, determining whether or not a person is "at" their computer (by detecting if keys are being depressed or the mouse is moving), and how much time in a given time period they were using their computer

For better or worse, virtually every activity on a user's computer can be recorded, either by gathering information from installed mainstream applications and the operating system, or from programs specifically installed to monitor user activities.

Using technology to monitor employee activity is fraught with a range of HR, legal, policy, ethical, and other issues. At a minimum, however, organizations need to be aware of the existence of the information created by employees in the course of using company-provided technology. Because, whether you like it or not, such information is likely to be used by the other side in litigation and investigations to the extent that they can find it and it reveals incriminating activity.

Furthermore, whether an organization chooses to use such technology or not, organizations need to be aware of the existence of monitoring tools. Organizations in the past have discovered such tools being used by competitors to spy on their activities and in the context of other damaging circumstances.

Notes

[1] *Qualcomm, Inc. v. Broadcom Corp.*, 2008 U.S. Dist. LEXIS 911 (S.D. Cal. Jan. 7, 2008).

[2] "Federal Judge Appoints WorldCom Monitor," Reuters, July 3, 2002.

[3] *State ex rel. Dispatch Printing Co. v. City of Columbus*, 90 Ohio St. 3d 39 (Ohio, 2000).

[4] "Contract to shred documents doesn't trump records law," *The News Media & The Law*, Fall 2000 (Vol. 24, No. 4), Page 35.

[5] Rosencrance, Linda, "InstallShield sues competitor Wise Solutions for electronic espionage," *Computerworld*, July 18, 2003.

[6] CERT® Advisory CA-1993-10 Anonymous FTP Activity.

[7] IRS Revenue Procedure 97-22 Section 4.

[8] Ibid., Section 5.

[9] Ibid., Section 7.

[10] *Toussie v. County of Suffolk*, 2007 U.S. Dist. LEXIS 93988 (E.D.N.Y. Dec. 21, 2007).

[11] *Zubulake v. UBS Warburg LLC*, 229 F.R.D. 422 (S.D.N.Y. 2004).

[12] Available at http://www.abanet.org/scitech/ec/isc/pag/pag.html

[13] These seven principles are: Notice, Choice, Onward Transfer, Security, Data Integrity, Access, and Enforcement.

[14] "Safe Harbor Privacy Principles," U.S. Department of Commerce, July 21, 2000.

[15] "Safe Harbor FAQ 7—Verification," U.S. Department of Commerce. Online at http://www.export.gov/safeharbor/Faq7verifFINAL.htm

[16] *Garrity v. John Hancock Mut. Life Ins. Co.*, 146 Lab. Cas. (CCH).

[17] Ibid.

[18] Study Highlights, Business Software Alliance/IDC Fifth Annual Global Software Piracy Study, May, 2008, available at http://global.bsa.org/idcglobalstudy2007/studies/highlights_globalstudy07.pdf.

Key #6

Effective and Consistent Program Enforcement

Information Management program policies and procedures must be consistently enforced through appropriate disciplinary mechanisms and the proper configuration and management of Information Management–related systems.

Key Overview

> The existence of a compliance program is not sufficient, in and of itself, to justify not charging a corporation for criminal conduct undertaken by its officers, directors, employees, or agents. Indeed, the commission of such crimes in the face of a compliance program may suggest that the corporate management is not adequately enforcing its program.

"Federal Prosecution of Corporations," U.S. Department of Justice[1]

Key #5 addressed the need for organizations to employ Information Management auditing and monitoring programs to measure compliance and detect program violations. This section explores what happens next: Once violations are detected, how should they be dealt with?

17 Addressing Employee Policy Violations

IMC recognizes that employees will violate policies and procedures. In some cases, they will do it willfully, despite being fully aware of the consequences. In other cases, violations result from an organization's failure in some aspect of its Information Management program development and implementation.

The reasons that Information Management program violations occur and vary include the following:

- **Lack of awareness**. Employees were unaware of the policy or procedure, because of inadequate communication and dissemination.
- **Confusion**. Employees were confused about what the policy meant or which policy applied to them, as a result of changes in organizational structure, changes in job roles and responsibilities, undue complexity, lack of training, or other factors.
- **Inconsistent enforcement and lack of oversight**. Policies were not consistently enforced, so employees believed they did not have to comply with them.
- **Willful acts**. Employees deliberately violated the policy out of self-interest and/or criminal intent.

Make Sure Employees Understand the Consequences

Organizations must be crystal clear with employees about the consequences of violating Information Management policies and procedures. Statements outlining consequences should be a standard part of the policies to which they relate, and should be highlighted, communicated, and re-communicated. In other words, these statements should become a standard part of the corporate culture of which every employee is keenly aware.

SAMPLE CONSEQUENCES POLICY STATEMENT

VIOLATION OF ANY ASPECT OF THIS POLICY MAY RESULT IN DISCIPLINARY ACTION, UP TO AND INCLUDING TERMINATION. Further, theft or assisting another in theft of any Company property, including Company Records, is a crime for which you may be criminally prosecuted. As such, you must read and follow this Policy, and seek clarification from your supervisor if you are unclear on any requirement. In addition, be aware that this Policy provides MINIMUM STANDARDS. Your department may provide additional and/or different directives that are required to ensure compliance with specific laws, regulations, and industry requirements.

© 2003, 2008, Randolph A. Kahn, ESQ., and Barclay T. Blair. For informational purposes only. Get the advice of counsel before adopting any Information Management policy element.

There are a variety of tools and techniques that organizations can use to help ensure that employees get the message. These include:

- Use an acknowledgment or certification process that requires employees to "sign off" that they have read and understood the policy, and understand the consequences of violating the policy.
- Inform employees that Information Management policies are subject to revision and updating.
- Provide a mechanism for employees to air grievances and seek clarifications related to the Information Management program.
- Consider how your organization will handle "whistleblowers" who bring violations to management's attention.

SAMPLE EMPLOYEE CERTIFICATION STATEMENT

Signing this document will certify that I have read and understand the *Records Management Manual*. I also understand that our Company is committed to protecting its Records and fully complying with all applicable laws and regulations. I will comply with any requirement to preserve Records pursuant to any Legal Hold Order or in conjunction with any audit, investigation, or litigation.

Inform Employees of Past Violations

It is important that organizations inform current employees of past violations of Information Management policies that have resulted in employee termination and other disciplinary actions. The reason for such communications is to provide a warning to all employees and to prevent further violations, not to embarrass or humiliate the employees who have been disciplined. Thus, these communications, whether in the form of an e-mail memo, verbal presentation, or other media, should be professional and focus on how employees can avoid similar situations.

- Do not use the disciplined employees' names, unless there is a very compelling reason to do so, and only with approval of the HR and Legal departments.
- Clearly describe the violation that took place, and if applicable, why it took place and the consequences to the employee.
- Refer to and/or quote the sections of company policy and/or laws that were violated.
- Describe the real or potential harm caused to the company by such violations.
- Describe what employees can do to avoid committing similar violations.
- Remind employees of the importance of the Information Management program as a whole.

The courts have made clear that not only do organizations have the right to communicate with their employees about such matters, but also it is in their interests to do so.

This idea was recently tested in *Garrity v. John Hancock Mut. Life Ins. Co.*,[2] where terminated employees sued their former employer for defamation after company supervisors told "former co-workers, and…employees in other departments, that plaintiffs were terminated for sending and receiving 'sexually lewd, harassing'…and 'sexually explicit' emails."

The court clarified that, even if the statements made by the supervisors rose to the level of defamation, the employer has the right to "disclose defamatory information about employees and former employees," including "an employer's statements of opinions and facts, and statements that an employer reasonably believes to be true."

The fired employees claimed that "no legitimate business purpose was served by disseminating these statements among such a large group of employees." However, the court disagreed, and stated:

> *To the contrary, all Hancock employees are subject to its email policy. Therefore, defendant had an obvious legitimate business purpose, as to all employees, if it so chose—to warn them and thereby prevent any recurrence of the events that led to this lawsuit.*

E-MAIL POLICY ENFORCEMENT

There are many cases in which organizations had good policies in place, but had no good system to ensure that their policies were followed.

For example, a global chemical company had a policy in place that prohibited use of the company e-mail system for sending, receiving, and viewing pornography and violent images. Following a complaint that workers were violating the e-mail policy by sharing pornography, among other prohibited content, the company was forced to fire about 50 experienced employees.

If the company had a good monitoring mechanism in place, the problem could have been identified before the violations were widespread, and one or two employees could have been disciplined—sending a message to the rest of the company and avoiding the disruption and scandal that ensued.

Enforcement Must Be Consistent

Consistency is central to effective Information Management program enforcement. Here's why:

- **Commitment**. Consistency tells employees that you are committed to the Information Management program, so, by implication, they too should be.
- **Clarity**. Consistency minimizes confusion about what will happen if policies are violated, thereby working to increase compliance.
- **Communication**. Consistency tells the outside world, including courts, regulators, auditors, and shareholders, that you take your Information Management obligations seriously.
- **Comfort**. Consistency helps to give customers and partners comfort in doing business with you.
- **Credibility**. Consistency makes enforcement easier for supervisors, managers, and the lawyers by making clear that the company does what it says it will do to ensure that employees do the right thing.
- **Fairness**. Consistency means all violators are treated equally, without favoritism or discrimination.

Although the benefits of consistent program enforcement are clear, many organizations continue to selectively enforce Information Management policies and procedures. While policies need to be somewhat flexible in order to be practical, variation from those directives must be reasonable and explainable.

For example, if an organization finds that employees are constantly violating its e-mail policy that requires them to keep their e-mail inboxes under a mandated size limit, the organization should investigate the cause, rather than simply turning a blind eye to the policy violation. Perhaps the limit is too restrictive, or the size issue is merely symptomatic of larger issues. Maybe employees are retaining too many e-mail messages, or are ignoring e-mail retention policies altogether. A failure to enforce formal written policy not only sends the wrong message to employees, but in this example, leads to increased storage cost and an increased chance that unnecessary e-mail messages will remain in the e-mail system long after they should have been disposed of in the ordinary course of business.

The Risks of Inconsistency

Establishing a consistent approach to enforcement helps to protect organizations from claims by accused violators that they are being selectively, unfairly, or discriminately singled out and disciplined while other violators are not disciplined for the same violation.

For example, in the employment action related to *Autoliv Asp v. Dep't of Workforce Servs*,[3] a state employment board was asked to consider whether or not two employees were terminated for just cause after they violated their employer's policies by sending sexually explicit and offensive e-mail messages through the company e-mail system.

The company's computer use policy specifically prohibited "use of email for reasons other than transmittal of business related information" and "conduct that reflects unfavorably on the corporation." In addition, the company had general rules of conduct and an anti-harassment policy that specified termination as a possible result of violation.

Before the employees were fired, the company had grown concerned about problems caused by excessive volume on the corporate e-mail system. Following an audit of e-mail use, the company determined that employees were using the system for a number of non-business-related activities. Following this discovery, the employer sent three company-wide e-mail notifications (including one from the VP of Human Resources), reminding employees that they were required to use the e-mail system only for business-related purposes, and that a failure to do so could result in termination.

Following a complaint from a former employee about receiving sexually harassing e-mail from current employees, the company investigated, found that two employees had sent a number of sexually explicit and offensive e-mail messages, and fired them for "improper and unauthorized use of company e-mail."

The terminated employees did not deny sending the e-mail messages but claimed that they were unaware that their conduct would result in termination. Subsequent hearings sided with the employees, in large part because the employer had inconsistently enforced their own e-mail policy.

For example, hearings related to the case found that,

- "Because the written policy against excessive email was not consistently enforced the claimants had no knowledge of the expected conduct."

- "Abuse of the company email was common among employees."
- "The company's strict written policy on email use differed from its actual application of that policy."[4]

The company had effectively shot itself in the foot. On the one hand, they had policies that were well thought out, and they effectively communicated those policies to employees. On the other hand, they had allowed the policies to be flagrantly violated for some time, likely because they had neither the resources nor inclination to take enforcement action, until they encountered a performance problem in the e-mail system. The inconsistent enforcement of their own policies enabled the terminated employees to raise doubt as to whether or not the policies were "real" and needed to be taken seriously, and thus dragged them into a legal battle in what should have otherwise been a straightforward case.

Common Inconsistencies

In our consulting practice we have the opportunity to see first-hand how organizations enforce their Information Management policies and practices. Our experience shows that there are many areas where organizations fail to enforce consistently. Some of these areas include:

1. **Special treatment for some**. In too many organizations, Information Management policies and practices simply don't seem to apply to some employees. For example, executives are sometimes allowed to delete e-mail messages that have Information Management significance, or are allowed to keep copies of e-mail in personal electronic and hard-copy archives long past their retention periods. While there may be some business justification for treating some executive e-mail differently from that of other employees on an ongoing basis, such treatment should be formally codified in policy and consistently enforced. In some cases, employees or entire departments are allowed to flout Information Management policies. The Marketing department exceeds e-mail mailbox sizes because they are sending around big presentations and graphics. The research department transmits big CAD files, and so on. While there may be a reason to vary the rules, generally the rules should be uniform across the company and then consistently enforced.

2. **"Unspoken" or de facto policies**. Some employees are allowed to purchase and use PDAs, messaging-enabled cell phones, and other devices on their own, despite a lack of policies addressing these technologies. In one company, the VP of sales had given his blessing to the sales team using a free P2P file sharing tool to share confidential sales presentations among the team, despite the fact that outsiders could hack into and download the presentations at will. Because of the ramifications caused by unofficial, off-policy practices, it is worthwhile to take the time to negotiate a real policy if one is needed.

3. **Neglected back-office operations**. Some companies seem to believe that what happens in the back-office doesn't affect Information Management. For example, we saw a company make an exception to its policy and allow its employees to overwrite backup tapes containing e-mail before the end of the retention periods, "just this once," simply because they had run out of backup tapes for that day's backup run. (As mentioned before, a company was penalized for this kind of activity in *Applied Telematics v. Sprint.*) In another case, the IT staff failed to overwrite e-mail backup tapes after the end of their retention periods. In *Murphy Oil USA, Inc. v. Fluor Daniel, Inc.*, the company had a 45-day retention period, but backup tapes containing 14 months of e-mail were found during discovery.

WHEN INCONSISTENCY BECOMES DISCRIMINATORY

Consider a scenario where a company has an Internet use policy that says Internet use should be for business purposes only. However, the company has turned a blind eye to frequent violations, as long as Internet access is not abused. A worker who returned from retirement is reprimanded for the time he spends searching the Web. In the policy violation review meeting that ensues, the elderly gentleman points out that "everyone" uses the Internet in violation of company policy, and he feels singled out because it takes him longer to read through online pages. If the company chose to formally discipline or even terminate him because of Internet overuse, he may be able to sue for age discrimination.

The courts have made clear that "discriminatory enforcement of a lawful policy is, of course, unlawful."[5]

Notes

[1] Memorandum of Deputy Attorney General Paul J. McNulty, "Federal Prosecution of Business Organizations," December 12, 2006.

[2] *Garrity v. John Hancock Mut. Life Ins. Co.*, 146 Lab. Cas. (CCH).

[3] *Autoliv Asp v. Dep't of Workforce Servs.*, 2001 UT App 198.

[4] Ibid.

[5] *Flynn v. Raytheon Co.*, 868 F. Supp. 383.

18 Using Technology to Enforce Policy

An organization's Information Management policies and procedures can be divided into those that require *manual* auditing, monitoring, and enforcement to ensure compliance, and those that can be *automatically* monitored and enforced using information technology. For example, an e-mail policy that restricts e-mail attachments to 2 MB can be enforced easily by configuring the e-mail server to reject larger attachments. In much the same way, a policy statement that requires employees to "encrypt all e-mail sent outside the company" clearly relies upon the proper configuration and management of an encryption system. If the system is not available or useable, employees cannot comply with the policy.

This section focuses on the latter category of policies and procedures, and explores techniques that all organizations should be aware of when endeavoring to ensure that such directives are effectively and consistently enforced.

Which Directives Can Be Automatically Enforced?

Organizations should anticipate the kinds of Information Management program violations they are likely to face, and how they will address such violations when they occur. An exercise that can be helpful in this regard is identifying those policy elements that can be enforced automatically through proper configuration and management of information technology. We use the term *automatically* with caution here, because all technology, no matter how advanced or sophisticated, still relies on humans for its proper configuration and management, even if it is as simple as just "flipping a switch."

New and powerful enterprise auditing and monitoring tools are continuously being developed. Those who have received calls from their credit card company after making an unusually large purchase using the card, or from their phone company after making an expensive long distance call across the world for the first time, can attest to this. These companies employ sophisticated monitoring technology that alerts personnel when unusual transactions occur within your account, effectively helping them enforce anti-fraud policies.

It is simply not feasible, though, to automatically track and enforce each employee's compliance with Information Management policies and procedures. After all, it is technically possible to create log files and other "electronic trails," which show how employees have been using company systems. It is another matter having the tools, people, and time to make sense of all that information.

Password policies are a great example—some aspects of which can be automatically enforced, and some of which cannot. For example, a good password policy should dictate the characteristics of allowable passwords, such as the following:

- Passwords must contain uppercase, lowercase, and numeric characters.
- Passwords must be at least six characters long.
- Passwords must not contain your username.

The software applications used to validate and accept network, e-mail, and other usernames and passwords can automatically enforce each of these policy elements. Thus, there is little need to manually audit or monitor user password formation, aside from ensuring that the software used to validate passwords is properly configured and operational.

However, there are common password policy elements that cannot be automatically enforced, so there is a need to monitor and audit compliance with those elements. For example, good password policies should address issues such as the following:

- Under no circumstances are employees allowed to share their password with anyone inside or outside the company, even if such sharing is to provide temporary access to a colleague or "cover" for someone out of the office.
- Passwords should never be written down, e-mailed, spoken, or communicated in any way to anyone inside or outside the company, including administrative assistants and managers.

- Passwords should not be based on personal information, such as date of birth, a child's or spouse's name, Social Security number, or any other information that could be easily guessed ("socially engineered") by someone who knows you or who has access to personal information about you.
- Passwords should never be displayed, stored, or concealed in your workspace.

Those policy elements cannot be automatically enforced by company systems. However, they are of equal, if not greater, importance to the company's overall information security program. Therefore, a company needs to develop a method to audit and monitor employee compliance with these directives that includes elements such as:

- Periodic manual review of a statistical sampling of employee passwords conducted by qualified and designated IT personnel
- Periodic inspection of a statistical sampling of employee's physical workspace to see if passwords are on display
- Periodic employee surveys regarding the use of passwords to gauge compliance

The following sections provide a number of sample policy elements and a discussion of how such elements may be automatically enforceable.

Sample Policy Element #1: E-Mail Content

All e-mail must be written in a professional manner, and should be free of profanity and sexually explicit content.

Automatically Enforceable?

To some extent.

How?

Although most people have at least an instinctive sense of what "written in a professional manner" means, it is sufficiently subjective that teaching it to a computer would be difficult. However, e-mail content filtering technology is readily available that can look for profanity, sexual language, and other triggers that might indicate that a message contains prohibited content.

This technology is used in many freely downloadable "spambusting" types of programs that are designed to identify and block spam. Aside from looking for specific words, these programs often use sophisticated Bayesian logic that looks at a wide variety of factors in making a determination about whether or not an e-mail is spam, including its size, content, sender, subject line formation, and other factors. The same basic technology can also be deployed on an enterprise-wide basis to block or quarantine suspect messages, thereby providing effective automatic enforcement of one element of a company's e-mail policy.

Sample Policy Element #2: Software Use

Employees are not allowed to download, install, or operate any software on company-supplied computers and devices that has not been supplied by the IT department. Unauthorized software can create security risks and legal liability issues for the company.

Automatically Enforceable?

Yes.

How?

Companies can use a variety of technologies and techniques to prevent all but the most sophisticated users from installing and using unauthorized software. For example, many operating systems can be configured to only allow IT administrators to install software. Operating systems can also be configured to only allow installation of software programs found on the company's network and not on the user's local hard drive. In addition, specialty programs can perform automatic auditing of a computer connected to the company network, and monitor and catalogue software used over the Internet or internal network. Although no method is foolproof, these technologies or techniques can help an organization enforce these kinds of policy elements.

Sample Policy Element #3: File Sharing and Instant Messaging

Employees are not allowed, under any circumstances, to use peer-to-peer (P2P) file sharing programs to download or upload files of any type from the

Internet or within the corporate network. Use of such technology may create security risks and subject the company to legal liability.

Automatically Enforceable?

Yes.

How?

Organizations can monitor the traffic flowing over their own networks and onto the Internet using a variety of tools and techniques, including firewalls and network/bandwidth monitoring software. These tools can be used to recognize and/or block certain types of network traffic, such as P2P file sharing applications. Organizations with policy elements preventing the use of specific communications technologies such as P2P file sharing and instant messaging, for example, can use these tools to automatically enforce compliance with such directives by controlling and/or blocking their use.

Similar techniques could also be used to block instant messaging traffic from leaving the company's internal network in order to enforce a policy element such as the following:

> Although the company provides Instant Messaging facilities for you to use, Instant Messaging is only to be used for communicating with other employees, and is never to be used to communicate with clients, partners, or any outside parties under any circumstance.

Sample Policy Element #4: Legal Hold

No documents, communications, or Records subject to Legal Hold may be altered, disposed of, erased, or otherwise made inaccessible, whether in paper or electronic form, for any reason whatsoever. Failure to preserve Business Information specified in a Legal Hold can subject the Company, its Associates, and third parties to fines, sanctions, criminal conviction, including being incarcerated, and other legal penalties.

Automatically Enforceable

No.

Why?

A Legal Hold is a complex process that may involve dozens, if not hundreds of employees and thousands of pieces of information that may have to be preserved. It should not be thought of as a policy element or process that is automatically enforceable using information technology. That being said, technology can play a big role in the Legal Hold process, such as:

- Using the corporate intranet to disseminate Legal Hold information to ensure that employees understand their preservation obligations.
- Preventing unauthorized destruction or alteration of responsive records.
- Collecting and preserving responsive records and other electronic information in electronic form.
- Copying responsive material from employee hard drives and network file locations.
- Finding and producing material from company databases, document management systems, Records Management software systems, and so on.

While Rule 37(e) of the Federal Rules of Civil Procedure provides that courts cannot impose sanctions upon a party for failure to provide electronically stored information lost as a result of the routine, good faith operation of an information system, the Advisory Committee notes emphasize that the loss of data must be in "good faith." "Good faith . . . may involve a party's intervention to modify or suspend certain features of that routine operation to prevent the loss of information, if that information is subject to a preservation obligation." Thus, the Federal Rules contemplate that a Legal Hold would *require* manual intervention in an information system.

Managing the Administrators

Let's face it: The more that an organization depends on information technology in its Information Management program, the more the organization relies on the talents, training, experience, and ethics of its IT staff and administrators. There is an entire realm of Information Management-related policies and procedures that specifically apply to the work that IT administrators do that also must be consistently enforced. And the people doing the enforcing have to be knowledgeable enough about the technology to make an accurate assessment of compliance.

After all, it is the "trusted insider" who is usually capable of causing the most harm in an organization, whether due to negligence, incompetence, or malicious intent. To put it another way, how does a company protect itself from someone who not only has all the keys to the building but also designed the locks? The more technology-savvy an employee, the more likely it is that they will be able to flout Information Management policies and procedures and get away with it.

TECH BOSSES NEED TO BE TECH-SAVVY

A flaw in the design and controls of an off-track betting system in New York for horse racing was recently exploited to the tune of $3 million. A delay between the time bets were made by bettors, and when bets were received and finalized by the central betting system, allowed an insider to change bets to name the winning horses of races that had already been run. Had the company's supervisors been as capable with the technology as the employee who recognized the flaw and exploited it, there is a good chance that the fraud could have been avoided.

As it pertains to information security specifically, there are a number of techniques used by organizations to minimize the amount of damage that a trusted insider would be capable of doing, such as requiring the collaboration of two or more parties for sensitive security operations. A well-designed program for hiring employees who will be given access to such sensitive information and processes should also be employed.

Organizations might have well-researched and well-written internal policies that dictate how IT administrators should configure and manage information technology, but these policies will do little good unless companies are able to ensure that IT staff is consistently applying these policies in the real world. Information technology touches nearly every aspect of Information Management in most companies today, which means that IMC largely relies on IT professionals to properly configure and manage IT systems.

Key #7

Continuous Program Improvement

When improper management of information is detected, the organization must take all reasonable steps to respond appropriately to the activity and to prevent further similar activities—including making any necessary modifications to its Information Management Program.

Key Overview

Continuous program improvement is the last of the Seven Keys to IMC. You must continuously improve and update your Information Management program and adapt it to changes in your business, new laws and regulations, and problems and weaknesses that are discovered through your auditing and monitoring programs.

19 The Ongoing Work of IMC

I f there is one overarching message that readers should take away from this book, it is that IMC is a *process*, not a *project*. The process of IMC can certainly be broken down into projects where much of the work is done in their initial phases (i.e., drafting policies and procedures), but even those activities require ongoing review, updating, and improvement.

Every organization must strive to continually improve its Information Management program. Every program has flaws and weaknesses that need to be addressed. Every program becomes out of date with current best practices, laws, and technology unless it is continuously revised and revisited. Every program can be better.

Why Is Continuous Program Improvement (CPI) Required?

Organizations must continue to update and change their Information Management program in order to ensure that it keeps doing its job. That job is to protect and promote the organization's legal and business interests.

While the specific drivers of change are always evolving, the reasons that organizations need to continuously improve their programs are relatively constant, and include:

- **Addressing flaws and failures**. Addressing flaws that were discovered through auditing and monitoring, flaws that were brought to the attention of the organization through a grievance process, and failures that blossomed into full-fledged legal or regulatory action.

- **Changing business focus**. Adapting to new business strategies, such as a shift from U.S. to European markets, might require a change in the approach to employee and customer privacy protection.
- **Changing technology**. Updating the program to anticipate Information Management issues raised by the use of new kinds of technology, such as instant messaging and P2P file sharing.
- **Changing laws and regulations**. Ensuring that program elements comply with new or updated laws and regulations. There have been many new laws and regulations affecting Information Management in recent years, and the pace of lawmaking does not appear to be slowing.
- **Changing best practices**. Best practices are constantly changing in every industry to account for changing market conditions and other factors, and this must be reflected in Information Management policies and practices. For example, while few organizations explicitly addressed e-mail issues in a separate policy, it has become a best practice to do so in organizations that rely heavily on e-mail for business purposes.
- **Changing levels of risk**. Companies started on the basis of new and innovative technologies may find their risk levels reduced as the technology becomes more mature. On the other hand, firms in established industries may face higher risk levels from changing market conditions (i.e., mortgage lenders may require more sophisticated credit-checking capabilities).

Changing Technology Means Changing the Program

We conclude that in today's workplace, the e-mail transmission of sexually explicit and offensive jokes, pictures, and videos constitutes a flagrant violation of a universal standard of behavior.

Autoliv Asp v. Dep't of Workforce Servs., 2001 UT App 198

At one time, e-mail use was largely limited to the world of research institutions and defense contractors. Then, with the growing popularity of the World Wide Web, students and other tech-savvy people around the world adopted it. Businesses began to catch on and see the potential of the technology. Over time, of course, the technology has become widespread, with nearly all organizations using it in some form, and many completely reliant on it.

Unfortunately, even as businesses invested heavily in e-mail technology, most did not show the same enthusiasm for updating and adapting Information Management program policies and procedures to account for the technology. As a result, an avalanche of court cases and legal actions related to the use and misuse of e-mail began, and organizations were forced to retroactively change their Information Management practices. Many learned their lesson the hard way, feeling the pain of harassment lawsuits and mass employee terminations.

Even today, as hard as it may be to believe, there are still a significant number of organizations that fail to address e-mail use in their Information Management policies and procedures. Nearly a quarter of organizations surveyed in the AIIM/KCI survey do not provide employees with formal written policies regarding e-mail, for example.

A PRESCRIPTION FOR PAIN

In our consulting practice we came across a pharmaceutical company that had implemented an employee PDA program in which every employee in the company received a handheld device with software that had been specifically customized for the firm. It was cutting-edge, visionary, and everyone was excited—except the Compliance department. Actually, the Compliance department didn't feel any emotions about the PDA program because they were not consulted at all.

Several months later, the cutting-edge program was deemed a success. The employees were hooked and had incorporated the handy little devices into almost every aspect of their working lives.

Then the FDA came knocking. And asked troubling compliance questions.

"Can you explain to us how these PDAs comply with FDA recordkeeping requirements? How and where exactly is the information on these PDAs retained? How is it protected?"

The program was scrapped. Millions of dollars were wasted.

The company failed horribly in the way they implemented the program, but at least they did one thing right. They realized that the most effective way to "continuously improve" the program was to get rid of it.

Which Technology Is Next?

Have organizations around the world learned their lesson, or are they doomed to repeat the mistakes of the past by implementing new technology without adequate consideration of its Information Management obligations? Only time will tell.

Even a cursory glance at today's technology landscape quickly reveals that there are many technologies that appear to be taking a similar path.

Business use of instant messaging has become widespread enough to attract the attention of regulators like the National Association of Securities Dealers, which has told brokers that they need to supervise and retain instant messages like any other form of business correspondence.

Instant messaging has a variety of Information Management implications. Can messages be retained? Is it secure? Should we allow employees to use it to talk to customers, or should it only be for internal purposes? Can we be sued if someone tells a dirty joke via an instant message? Many of these issues are the same as e-mail, and organizations can certainly build on the work they have done in that area. On the other hand, instant messaging presents its own new set of challenges that organizations need to investigate and address, such as the inability to pre-review communications. The question is: Will they? Or will instant messaging provide the next wave of Information Management-related lawsuits?

P2P file sharing is another likely candidate. Aside from the security issues created by employees opening a hole in the corporate defenses to share MP3s of their favorite bands using consumer-oriented P2P tools, there are numerous other serious issues, including copyright infringement. One company has already publicly settled a copyright infringement action with the Recording Industry Association of America over the operation of an MP3 file-trading network inside the company. While P2P technology is also employed for a wide variety of legitimate business purposes, it creates Information Management issues that must addressed proactively.

Blogs should also be covered by an organization's Information Management policies. Blogs expose the organization to the same degree of liability as the organization's website, except that content can change much more rapidly via blog postings, the ability to comment upon blog posts serves as another point of vulnerability to spammers and hackers, and there may be many more corporate bloggers that the organization may need to monitor. As blog posts are very easy to publish, employees may occasionally forget that they are representatives of the company.

One study predicts that by 2009, 50% of organizations will use wikis as important collaboration tools.[1] Wikis are collaboration tools which every approved user can edit. The study recommended that wiki users understand each wiki's "code of conduct," and organizations must ensure that the rules are monitored and enforced. A champion for each wiki is recommended. Companies should be cognizant of their corporate culture when considering whether to implement wikis—companies with traditional hierarchical information dissemination practices may not adapt well to the use of wikis.

Changes in the technology used in your organization, regardless of how insignificant or informal they may seem today, demand changes in Information Management policies and procedures.

EVEN THE EXPERTS DON'T ALWAYS GET IT RIGHT

The U.S. General Accounting Office (GAO) reviewed the way the National Archives and Records Administration (NARA), our nation's keeper of records, was going about acquiring a system to manage and store electronic records.

NARA had created a plan for acquiring an advanced electronic records archive (ERA) based on the "recognized industry standards set by the Institute of Electrical and Electronics Engineers,"[2] one of the primary standards bodies in the digital world.

However, the GAO found that "key policy and planning documents are missing elements that are required by the standards," resulting in "serious long-term risks to the costs, schedule, and performance."

As a result, NARA's "Chief Information Officer" was required to "take a range of actions" designed to address the shortfalls, including "revising key planning documents."

Dealing with Flaws and Failure

Organizations must have a mechanism in place to deal with Information Management program failures. Failures will happen, and they provide an opportunity for organizations to learn and improve their programs and avoid the mistakes of the past.

Find the True Source of the Failure

Sometimes events that appear to be the cause of a program failure are actually a symptom of a larger problem, so it is important that organizations ensure that they have found the true source of the problem when designing program improvements.

For example, a client recently told us that they had been considering a major investment in network equipment and additional bandwidth to resolve an ongoing problem with a slow corporate network and Internet access that routinely "bogged down." However, before they made the purchase, a member of their IT staff installed and ran a network monitoring program. The program revealed that dozens of employees were using P2P file sharing software, with many employees constantly downloading files over the Internet from the time they got into work until the time they left. The client informed employees that file sharing was not allowed at work, and network performance shortly improved to the point that the additional investment was not required.

Do not assume that violations of Information Management policies are isolated incidents. If one employee is not properly retaining electronic records or is routinely failing to encrypt confidential e-mail messages, for example, it is possible that others are committing the same violation, and such patterns should be investigated through Information Management auditing and monitoring programs.

Take Disciplinary Action

Organizations need to be swift, decisive, and consistent when addressing violations of Information Management policies and practices. Tell employees what will happen if they violate policies and procedures. If employees commit a violation, use the event to learn where your Information Management program may be lacking, and ask hard questions about it. Was the employee properly trained? Could the policy be any clearer? Do we need to communicate more regularly with employees about their Information Management obligations? Use the insights you gain from such incidents to improve your program and minimize the likelihood of such failures occurring again.

Correct the Problem

Correcting Information Management problems is often much more difficult than disciplining a few employees and updating a few policies. In fact,

Information Management problems are often systemic and can only be addressed through a complete reexamination of the organization's overall approach. Failures that are related to "big picture" issues, such as a poorly functioning organizational structure or a lack of executive support, extend beyond Information Management specifically and need to be addressed in a different context.

Not every problem is so complex, however. Some problems can be addressed through relatively minor changes to policies or procedures, or by investing in new technology or reconfiguring existing technology. For example, network- and bandwidth-monitoring technology can be a great ally in your effort to enforce policies governing how employees use the Internet, and can be an affordable addition to your arsenal of program enforcement and improvement tools.

Change and Improvement Is Always Needed

With the rush to go electronic, some state and local governments put public records on the Web without first creating policies addressing which records need to be there. After 9/11, that decision has to be revisited in recognition that having certain records online (including architectural plans for buildings) enhances the risk of a terrorist attack. As a result, policy is developed and public records are evaluated on a case-by-case basis to determine what belongs online.

Provide a Mechanism for Inquiries

Any program that requires employee compliance must provide a mechanism for employees to ask questions, seek clarification, and address problems. The Information Management program is no different. Some of the most insightful and useful information about the functioning of the program is likely to come from the people who are applying it every day in a variety of situations that may or may not have been contemplated by the program architects. Remind employees often how they can communicate with the organization about the program, and regularly encourage them to do so (or even reward them for doing so).

CHANGE MANAGEMENT: THE KEY TO SUCCESS IN IMPLEMENTING PROGRAM IMPROVEMENTS

Change Management is an important aspect of Continuous Program Improvement because at its core, Change Management seeks to address the people aspect of any project or program enhancement. The goal of the organization's Change Management is to ensure the success of program changes by assessing and addressing the impact of those changes on affected groups and individuals. An Information Management program that fails to address Change Management greatly increases its risk of failure.

Characteristics of unsuccessful projects often include one or more of the following:

- Lack of project alignment with overall business strategy
- Poor business requirements identification
- Insufficient buy-in and support from senior management
- Incomplete understanding of how the changes will affect key stakeholder groups (i.e., "what's in it for me?")
- Poor communication about the change within the organization, including impacts and benefits
- Failure to budget sufficient resources to address process, communications, and training requirements

To ensure your Information Management program succeeds, it is critical that you closely analyze and address its impact on your employees who play a critical role in making the program successful.

Strategies for Success

There are a number of Change Management strategies that the organization can implement to increase the success of its Information Management program changes and updates.

Here is a list to get you started:

Know your stakeholders. An Information Management program affects individuals and groups in different ways. It is imperative that you take the time to identify the key stakeholders affected by the change, how they will be impacted, and what the benefits of the change are to them. Don't forget to spend the time to analyze stakeholders that are against your program.

CHANGE MANAGEMENT: THE KEY TO SUCCESS IN IMPLEMENTING PROGRAM IMPROVEMENTS *(Continued)*

You will need to think about how to either change the mindset of these stakeholders to support your program, or determine how best to neutralize their ability to slow down/stop your program.

Conduct a high-level gap analysis. Think about the vision of your Information Management program. What does excellence look like? How would the company act under the new program? What processes would be in place? What new roles would need to be established? How would individuals and groups need to change their work habits? What efficiencies/costs savings/cost avoidance would result? Areas to consider include the following:

- New roles and responsibilities
- New procedures and processes
- New tools and systems
- New training and job aids
- New governance models
- New measurements and rewards

Once you've thought about the future (the "To-Be"), identify the gaps (the "As-Is"). Look at some of the key stakeholder groups and, using the focus areas, identify where they are today. By comparing today's world and the future vision you will be able to begin planning the journey.

Develop a compliance management "change roadmap." There's a reason people use maps when they travel in unfamiliar territory. The map helps them identify a route from point "A" to point "B," track their progress along the journey, and adjust as issues and problems arise (road construction, detours, and so on). If you have done a gap analysis the "As-Is" is your starting point; the "To-Be" is your destination.

For each significant stakeholder group you will need a high-level roadmap. Identify tangible tasks/activities that will need to happen to make the change successful for that particular audience.

Once you've completed your group analysis, consolidate your findings into an overall roadmap that summarizes the broad impacts on the organization.

Continues

CHANGE MANAGEMENT: THE KEY TO SUCCESS IN IMPLEMENTING PROGRAM IMPROVEMENTS (*Continued*)

Construct a solid business case. You cannot establish a sense of urgency and interest in your compliance program without the facts. First, make sure your business case aligns with your corporate strategy. This will help greatly when you are getting executive buy-in to the business case. Second, the business case needs to address both quantitative and qualitative reasons for implementing a compliance management program—focus wherever possible on things that tangibly impact the company's bottom-line financials. Cost avoidance (reduced risk of litigation), quicker access to information, efficient reuse of corporate knowledge, and compliance with governmental regulations are all examples of this. Third, do not forget to develop a risk analysis as part of the business case so that people clearly understand the risks involved in the program and how you plan to mitigate these risks. Finally, make sure your business case has a post-implementation measurements process to ensure the benefits you have established in your business case are achieved.

Establish buy-in and leverage "change champions." Change champions play a critical role both in the compliance management planning/approval process, as well as the implementation. During the approval process you should identify, for each of the key stakeholder groups, respected individuals with whom you can review your overall business case and change impacts and get feedback. Try to find individuals who can be used as "references" in support of the program. After gathering this feedback, adjust the roadmap/stakeholder analysis and business case to reflect this feedback.

Once implementation begins, it's critical to directly involve representatives from the key stakeholder groups in the change program. Try to draw upon those individuals that you spoke with when gaining support for your business case. Prior to identifying these champions, make sure you can set expectations around their roles/responsibilities. These individuals will need to:

- Provide guidance, insight, and perspective to your implementation, including review of selected deliverables and feedback on stakeholder group buy-in, communications strategies, and implementation

CHANGE MANAGEMENT: THE KEY TO SUCCESS IN IMPLEMENTING PROGRAM IMPROVEMENTS (*Continued*)

- Help in the communications process—leveraging the champions to communicate to their respective groups will lend additional credibility to your change program
- Participate on any project working committees

Make sure you also try to estimate a time commitment for the champion, for example 2 to 4 hours per week. This will help to establish expectations and ensure that the right champions participate in the work effort.

Create a comprehensive communications plan. Communicate and communicate again. That being said, communicating smartly and targeting your messages requires thoughtful planning and analysis. See if you can leverage a communications professional within your company as a guide. They can look at your stakeholder analysis and identify key messages, different communications pathways, and the timing of your messages. Don't forget to have as part of the plan a feedback mechanism—have in place different means for getting feedback from your stakeholders and to measure the success of your change efforts.

Identify one or two quick wins to generate positive support and feedback. Is there something in your existing compliance management process that you can change in order to declare an early victory as well as demonstrate your program can generate the agreed-upon benefits? Look for "low hanging fruit," i.e., wins that will generate quick value within a short amount of time and with a small amount of money/resources expended. Early celebration of success and recognition of those individuals/groups involved will build momentum and help increase overall program buy-in.

Evaluate the success or failure of the change with the program sponsor and appropriate change champions. Once you have implemented the program, aggressively focus on benefits realization. Monitor the success metrics established in the business case and make sure that you are achieving the benefits promised. If not, work closely with the program sponsor and appropriate change champions to analyze the issues and make corrections. Change journeys hit a wall that you will need to break through—use your plans and persistence to overcome these post-implementation obstacles and to make your compliance management program a long-term success.

Courtesy of James Hospodarsky, Director of Global Knowledge Management, Dimension Data Holdings plc

Communicating Flaws and Failures ───

Communicating about Information Management program failures can be tricky business. On the one hand, communicating about weaknesses and failures helps bring the problem to the forefront and sends a message that the organization is committed to solving their problems. On the other hand, admissions of failure can open up an organization to legal liability. Organizations must determine the correct approach on a case-by-case basis. In addition, as explored below, there may be occasions where disclosure may be required by law.

The concept of "corporate accountability and transparency" has become popular in the wake of the many high-profile corporate scandals of the opening years of the new century. The expectation of shareholders and citizens, and indeed of the drafters of laws like Sarbanes-Oxley, is that organizations will be more forthcoming about the problems they face and the risks they represent. They expect greater disclosure of internal problems, and they expect that incompetence will be immediately corrected and fraud will be swiftly and harshly punished.

COMPETITIVE INFORMATION

The self-critical analysis privilege is only one of the many principles that are used to prevent the disclosure of certain internal company records. For example, companies often argue that revealing certain internal information should be protected because it would benefit competitors if publicly released during legal proceedings.

This principle was tested in Oregon in 2003, where the jury in an antitrust lawsuit found a large lumber firm guilty of anti-competitive behavior, and awarded nearly $80 million in damages to a small sawmill company. The company argued that certain records used in the trial should not be publicly released, as they would help competitors, but the court ruled that the public interest overcame the company's concerns.

The documents included memos that discussed various aspects of the company's success in the market, and even included a PowerPoint presentation allegedly predicting timeframes for the demise of competitive sawmills—damaging information in the context of antitrust litigation.

Communication May Be Required by Law

There are occasions where organizations will be compelled by law to disclose failures to the public. For example, Sarbanes-Oxley requires a public company's CEO and CFO to certify in each annual and quarterly report that they have reviewed the report, and that the information in the report is true, does not omit important information, and is not misleading. This is a law that appears to require public companies to communicate certain failures.

Another example is SB 1386, a law that went into effect in the state of California in July 2003. The California law requires organizations to notify the public about security breaches. More specifically, it requires any organization "that owns or licenses computerized data that includes personal information… disclose any breach of the security of the data." The law was developed largely in response to an incident in which hackers accessed California state government computers that contained information on over 200,000 state employees, after which the government took weeks to notify the employees about the incident.

Since the enactment of the California law, 43 states, the District of Columbia, and Puerto Rico have enacted laws requiring notification for security breaches.[3]

Failure under the law may give rise to lawsuits and monetary damages. Put another way, now companies that do business with California residents, or have their information, not only have to properly manage their personal information but may also have to protect against malicious hackers criminally gaining access to personal information through inadequately secured company computers.

Aside from liability issues, organizations are typically reluctant to provide information on hacking incidents as it may reveal valuable information to competitors about the organization's approach to data management and about its investments in information technology. The effect of SB 1386 on these types of disclosures will be instructive and organizations should watch the development of practices around this law closely.

Notes

[1] Brad Kenney, "Seven Strategies for Implementing a Successful Corporate Wiki," *Industry Week*, January 25, 2008.

[2] "National Archives and Records Administration's Acquisition of Major System Faces Risks," *GAO Highlights*, August 2003.

[3] McAfee, Inc. Solution Brief, "Understanding Today's Privacy Regulations," 2008; available at `http://www.mcafee.com/us/local_content/solution_briefs/sb_understanding_privacy_regulations.pdf`

Conclusion

We are in a business environment where information plays an increasingly important role in the success of both public and private organizations. In our imperfect world, where information is contemporaneously growing in volume and importance, we have ample evidence to take Information Management seriously. In recent times, we have seen IMC failures take a huge toll on countless companies that mismanaged or entirely failed to manage their information assets.

Companies have withered away. State and federal governmental institutions have obliterated already limited budgets trying to comply with recordkeeping laws. Corporations have been suffering through an ample amount of bad press for information mismanagement. And company employees have been accused, convicted, and incarcerated for IMC failures.

We have witnessed a confluence of events that makes a compelling case that what organizations have been doing up to this point may not be good enough. Policies drafted but not enforced can mean failure. The existence of an Information Management program, but inconsistent application of its directives can mean failure. Developing the directives, but improperly delegating responsibility for their implementation and enforcement, can mean failure. Failing to tell employees to refrain from destroying "anything potentially relevant" or suspending the records retention schedule in the context of an impending lawsuit can also mean failure. Responsibility to prevent these failures begins at the top of organizations and trickles down to all employees.

Successful Information Management today requires a discipline that to this point has been used almost exclusively by the compliance community. IMC is a methodology that applies a compliance framework to all Information Management and is designed to increase the chances that your organization will get it right or provide some insulation when it does not. A half-hearted or unsupported Information Management effort is not good enough. Information Management needs to be done right. We believe IMC and our Seven Keys provide a methodology to help you and your organization get it right.

Mistakes will happen—they always do. IMC is about building an Information Management environment where less can go wrong. It is also about building an environment that minimizes the costs and harm when things do go wrong. Our hope is that Information Management Compliance will also provide you and your organization with the benefit of the doubt by courts, regulators, bosses, stockholders, and the public when failure strikes. Our hope is that our Seven Keys will help you, and your organization, be more successful.

Index